Lecture Notes of the Institute for Computer Sciences, Social Informatics and Telecommunications Engineering 380

More information about this series at http://www.springer.com/series/8197

Yu Weng · Yuyu Yin · Li Kuang ·
Zijian Zhang (Eds.)

Tools for Design, Implementation and Verification of Emerging Information Technologies

15th EAI International Conference, TridentCom 2020
Virtual Event, November 13, 2020
Proceedings

 Springer

Editors
Yu Weng
Minzu University of China
Beijing, China

Li Kuang
Central South University
Changsha, China

Yuyu Yin
College of Computer
Hangzhou Dianzi University
Hangzhou, China

Zijian Zhang
Beijing Institute of Technology
Haidian, Beijing, China

ISSN 1867-8211   ISSN 1867-822X (electronic)
Lecture Notes of the Institute for Computer Sciences, Social Informatics
and Telecommunications Engineering
ISBN 978-3-030-77427-1   ISBN 978-3-030-77428-8 (eBook)
https://doi.org/10.1007/978-3-030-77428-8

This Springer imprint is published by the registered company Springer Nature Switzerland AG
The registered company address is: Gewerbestrasse 11, 6330 Cham, Switzerland

Preface

We are delighted to introduce the proceedings of the 15th European Alliance for Innovation (EAI) International Conference on Testbeds and Research Infrastructures for the Development of Networks and Communities (TridentCom 2020), which was held virtually on November 13, 2020. This conference brought together technical experts and researchers from academia and industry from all around the world to discuss the science and application of testbeds for big data, cyber-physical systems, and the emerging technologies in networking and communications.

The technical program of TridentCom 2020 consisted of 12 full papers, which were presented in two sessions: Session 1 - Computer Network and Testbed Application, and Session 2 - Analytics for Big Data of Images and Test.

Coordination with the steering chairs, Imrich Chlamtac, Victor C. M. Leung, and Honghao Gao, was essential for the success of the conference. We sincerely appreciate their constant support and guidance. It was also a great pleasure to work with such an excellent organizing committee team, we are grateful for their hard work in organizing and supporting the conference. In particular, we would like to thank the Technical Program Committee (TPC), led by our TPC Co-chairs, Dr. Yuyu Yin and Dr. Zijian Zhang, who completed the peer-review process for the technical papers and put together a high-quality technical program. We are also grateful to all the authors who submitted their papers to TridentCom 2020.

We strongly believe that the TridentCom conference provides a good forum for all researchers, developers, and practitioners to discuss all science and technology aspects that are relevant to big data, cyber-physical systems, and computer communications. We also expect that future TridentCom conferences will be as successful and stimulating, as indicated by the contributions presented in this volume.

April 2021

Yu Weng
Yuyu Yin
Li Kuang
Zijian Zhang

Organization

Steering Committee

Imrich Chlamtac	University of Trento, Italy
Victor C. M. Leung	The University of British Columbia, Canada
Honghao Gao	Shanghai University, China

Organizing Committee

General Chairs

Yu Weng	Minzu University of China, China
Li Kuang	Central South University, China

Program Chairs

Zijian Zhang	Beijing Institute of Technology, China
Yuyu Yin	Hangzhou Dianzi University, China

Workshop Chair

Guosheng Yang	Minzu University of China, China

Publicity and Social Media Chair

Ruoyu Chen	Beijing Information Science & Technology University, China

Publication Chair

Wenmin Lin	Hangzhou Dianzi University, China

Local Arrangement Chair

Weng Yu	Minzu University of China, China

Web Chair

Xiaoxian Yang	Shanghai Second Polytechnic University, China

Technical Program Committee

Zijian Zhang	Beijing Institute of Technology, China
Yuyu Yin	Hangzhou Dianzi University, China
Xiaoxian Yang	SSPU, China
Fekade Getahun	Addis Ababa University, Ethiopia

Contents

Computer Network and Testbed
Application

Prototyping an SDN Control Framework for QoS Guarantees

Mohamed Rahouti[1]([✉]), Kaiqi Xiong[2], and Yufeng Xin[3]

[1] Fordham University, The Bronx, NY 10458, USA
mrahouti@fordham.edu
[2] University of South Florida, Tampa, FL 33620, USA
xiongk@usf.edu
[3] University of North Carolina, Chapel Hill, NC 27599, USA
yxin@renci.org

Abstract. The centralized control capability of Software-Defined Networking (SDN) gives us an excellent opportunity to enhance the Quality of Service (QoS) routing. The end-to-end QoS-aware traffic forwarding must consider the computation latency associated with optimal path selection while reducing the controller's response time. In this paper, we propose a new SDN controller framework that consists of a queueing mechanism, active link delay measurements, efficient statistic estimate of network states, and intelligent path computation and selection. We implement our framework as a modular application in a Floodlight SDN controller software and conduct comprehensive experimental studies on the Global Environment for Network Innovations (GENI) testbed. Our performance evaluation based on experimental results demonstrates that the proposed framework can significantly reduce the latency in both the control plane and data plane, and find optimal paths with the minimum end-to-end delay.

Keywords: Software-Defined Networking · OpenFlow · Global environment for networking innovations · Path selection · Latency · Queueing · Quality of Service

1 Introduction

Software-Defined Networking (SDN) has become a vital network paradigm for expediting network management and control. It provides a global view of network resources and separates its control layer from its infrastructure layer [5]. Via a logically centralized controller, an SDN permits programmable interfaces to insert and push forwarding rules into forwarding devices (e.g., Open vSwitch) flow table for efficient network communication [14]. In order to better leverage SDN capabilities, the delicate holistic view of flows must be regarded as contributory to networking applications (e.g., traffic engineering [5], QoS-aware flow routing [15,16], and flow inspection [6]).

Y. Weng et al. (Eds.): TridentCom 2020, LNICST 380, pp. 3–16, 2021.
https://doi.org/10.1007/978-3-030-77428-8_1

Various research studies have been carried out to explore and enhance the Quality of Service (QoS) in SDN environments. The majority of previous studies have shed light on the data plane latency performance in terms of packet trip time. The end-to-end latency involves multiple factors, including propagation delay, switching latency, and control plane latency. It is important to note that the data-control communication delay (i.e., the delay associated with sending packets from a switch to the controller and back/OpenFlow packet_ins and packet_outs) plays a significant role in the end-to-end delay of traffic delivery. Therefore, the centralized control of networking traffic in SDN networks presents an additional factor that can not be ignored in designing latency control mechanisms.

To ensure QoS, a typical solution can be the dedication of more resources, such that the controller's response time is reduced. However, such a solution may significantly increase the complexity and operational cost of the infrastructure (e.g., energy and consumption cost). Moreover, the processing resources of SDN controllers at the service provider (SP) can be limited (i.e., SP restricts the concurrent virtual machine instances per account), where application-specific QoS may be adversely degraded. Thus, it is essential to note that the stability of QoS is crucial as it dominates the cost of infrastructural operation. Hence, aspects such as the controller response time (i.e., latency), flow rule processing, and forwarding delay have mutual dependencies, subsequently impacting the end-to-end communication delay and provisioned QoS. Therefore, it is of great interest to elaborate sophisticated processing and forwarding strategies at both the control and data planes to maintain QoS and optimize the operational cost without affecting the controller overheads (e.g., response time).

In this work, we address the end-to-end latency optimization problem of OpenFlow networks based on a systematic enhancement on both the control and data planes. Specifically, we leverage a prioritized service queueing model along with active measurements of the per-link latency mechanism to achieve optimization of per-flow end-to-end latency. Namely, the QoS mechanism we present is based on real-time per-link latency estimation and selects forwarding paths with minimal delay based upon an adaptive heuristic approach.

We implemented the proposed mechanisms in the Floodlight controller software. We then carried out comprehensive experiments in a live SDN network built in the GENI testbed to validate the proposed solution's efficiency. The experimental results demonstrate that our design model guarantees a significant improvement in end-to-end delay and controller response times.

Our contributions in this study are outlined as follows.

- Integration of controller's statistics into the design of a real-time end-to-end latency metric estimation and path selection.
- Adaptation of a queueing scheme to optimize controller's response time.
- Prototype and validation of the proposed approach in the multiple sites GENI testbed.

The rest of this paper is organized as follows. In Sect. 2, we further summarize existing studies and related work. Building upon this, in Sect. 3, we present a QoS model and respective architectural design of the SDN framework to resolve our research problem. In Sect. 4, we table validation methodologies of our proposed solution along with corresponding experimental findings. Finally, we conclude the paper discussion with future work in Sect. 5.

2   Related Work

In networking-enabled environments, QoS is regarded as the qualitative mensuration of networking services' overall performance, such as end-to-end communication delay [5]. Carrying out reliable QoS in SDN networks is of an essential benefit to providing dependable and efficient communication services and networking applications [17]. Thus, many recent studies have addressed the performance of OpenFlow devices. Yet, they have not provided effective solutions aligning in tandem with applications that require stringent optimization at both the control and data planes.

Most notably, some studies such as Huang et al. [10] and Rotsos et al. [19] studied the performance of SDN switching over various OpenFlow device vendors, whereas Curtis et al. [7] presented a notable mechanism to improve controller response times and switching delays. Over and above these studies, others tried to improve QoS guarantees in SDN networks using different approaches. Namely, Egilmez et al. [8] proposed an OpenFlow mechanism by leveraging the end-to-end bandwidth allocation for multimedia streaming, whereas Sharma et al. [20] and Celenlioglu and Mantar [4] presented SDN frameworks by leveraging open source controller software. The solution presented in [4] also tried to improve routing scalability and resource management, which subsequently enhances QoS guarantees in stationary nodes.

Other studies such as Jinyao et al. [22], Tariq and Bassiouni [21], and Hussain et al. [11] also tried to improve end-to-end communication QoS in SDN networks. Specifically, Jinyao et al. [22] leveraged queuing schemes for managing resource and bandwidth allocation along with an adjusted version of the Dijkstra algorithm to minimize delays in traffic delivery. Similarly, Tariq and Bassiouni [21] a multi-path-TCP (MPTCP) solution (for simulated SDN-enabled data centers) based upon best paths pre-computation between end-user nodes. Lastly, Hussain et al. [11] assessed a mechanism for hashed multi-path search in Floodlight controller software [1], where traffic scheduling and forwarding is performed via a hash function flow balancing service. Now since SDN controllers provide global traffic monitoring capabilities, various traffic engineering (TE) implementations also deploy these capabilities to enhance communication QoS. Namely, Google interconnected data centers (using SDN) while balancing capacity utilization of networks based upon application-specific priority [12]. Agarwal et al. [3] also tried to improve traffic delays and packet losses in environments interconnecting both OpenFlow and traditional routing devices. Furthermore, Jarschel et al. [13] tabled application-aware traffic management using Deep Packet Inspection (DPI) techniques. Further studies such as [23] resolved multimedia streaming QoS based upon a multi-priority flow scheme, such that high priority traffic is temporarily rerouted following congestion occurrence.

It is important to note that many past studies focused on TE in OpenFlow networks for QoS-enabled queueing tried to identify data plane traffic by port number with low accuracy (or even simply assume network can classify incoming traffic). Therefore, these solutions become impractical for real-world SDN environments. Furthermore, the majority of these summarized solutions have been tested over simulated experiments with impractical QoS criteria. To the best of our knowledge, none of these studies have proposed a practical SDN-enabled framework based upon combining and integrating a priority-based data-control queueing mechanism along with TE techniques to optimize the control response time and end-to-end traffic delay.

Nevertheless, despite these contributions, various open challenges remain here. For example, there is a further need to leverage the real-time data collection/processing capabilities and queueing mechanisms (at both the controller and OpenFlow switch) to achieve more effective traffic forwarding and dynamic path computation. This is indeed of particular importance to real-time traffic flows with tight delay QoS bounds (which can easily be impacted by time-varying bursty traffic). Furthermore, there is also a need to support priority queueing for multiple traffic levels in SDN networks. These data plane traffic priorities also need to be adequately integrated with SDN control plane traffic. Building upon the framework presented in [18], we propose an extended prototyping design with enhanced mechanisms to better improve the end-to-end QoS for traffic delivery with optimized controller's response time. Consider the design details presented next.

3   Design and Implementation

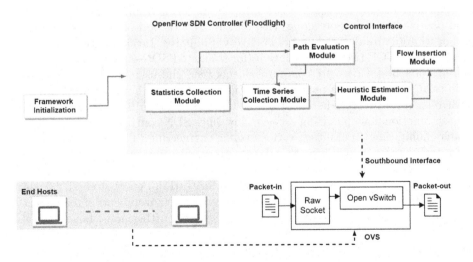

Fig. 1. Architectural design of the proposed framework.

In this work, the end-to-end communication scenario is contemplated in an SDN network, and the end nodes send and receive flows at a fixed rate across the networking environment. We are specifically concerned about communication delays, where the switch-controller communication (i.e., switch to controller channel), topology statistics calculation, and paths update are contributing factors in the packet forwarding delays [24]. In SDN delay-centric applications (i.e., applications that require low latency), an efficient flow forwarding mechanism must try to optimize the average end-to-end delay. Therefore, providing a close-to-optimal end-to-end delay for these applications is of great importance here to ensure efficient usage of link capacity and resources [5]. We develop an SDN mechanism by leveraging specific queueing mechanisms and traffic engineering techniques to address the presented challenges. Consider the details next.

The proposed framework architecture/modules are depicted in Fig. 1 and consists of four main modules, traffic classifier (queuing scheme), statistics collector, time series estimator, and optimal path selection. Modules are described and detailed in the following subsections.

3.1   Traffic Classifier and Queue Assignment

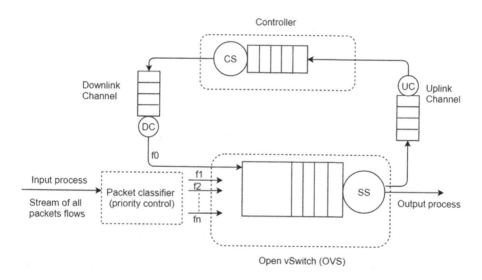

Fig. 2. The prioritized service-enabled queueing scheme for a data-control communication channel.

Many researchers have modeled the data plane as a Jackson network while the SDN controller as a finite queue. The shortcoming in such a model is that the model treats both control flows and data plane flows with an equal priority (i.e., normal networking traffic). According to recent studies, unlike SDN controllers, OpenFlow switches provide a reliable processing capacity of packets and forward packets in a microsecond. Moreover, an SDN controller is likely not to completely process *packet_in* messages with a very high arrival rate even when the processing time of a *packet_in* message may be few milliseconds (e.g., the arrival rate is bigger than thousands of packets per second).

The design of our proposed framework further relies upon an integrated set of queues. Namely, the uplink channel (UC) and downlink channel (DC) queues for switch-to-control and control-to-switch control packets buffering. Such queues are assumed to be of an infinite length. Moreover, the controller consists of a finite length queue to buffer arriving Packet_Ins/lookup requests. Meanwhile, the SDN-enabled switch implements a set of priority-based queues for incoming user flows buffering (after classification). Specifically, four priority levels are enabled here, i.e., normal, low, medium, and high. The control plane queues (DC, UC, and controller) are designed for management and control of flow rules, whereas the respective data plane queues buffer data packets with different priority levels. Finally, it is important to note that our framework's control packets are prioritized over data plane flows regardless of the latter's priority level. Therefore, throughout packet scheduling, control plane flows (i.e., in the control channel queue) are ensured a minimal delay of processing. In contrast, the data plane flows are handled according to their arrival priority levels.

Furthermore, when a new packet arrives in the switch, the switch-controller communication channel causes more latency towards the end-to-end packet delay. Therefore, a not-matched packet with existing flow rules can affect the rigorous end-to-end delay bound more than matched packets. Thus, a prioritized service queueing scheme is implemented along with our SDN framework, as depicted in Fig. 2. A priority queue is implemented in the infrastructure layer to separate flows that match existing flow rules (i.e., a routing path already calculated) from new packet arrivals. Moreover, the classification module classifies incoming data packets (client flows) into multiple priority levels and then buffers them separately. Note that a feedback control signal is also utilized to design the efficient priority-based transmission of all enqueued data flows, i.e., with the SDN controller performing dynamic queue control, detailed in a later section.

As the OpenFlow standards do not provide specifications to assign and configure queues, our OpenFlow switch is set up to isolate and classify traffic by enqueuing them on a separate queue on the egress port. The assigned queue on the data plane has an associated QoS configuration, including the queue capacity and the enqueued traffic service rate.

The purpose behind implementing such a queueing scheme is to minimize the overall traffic delay (between a given pair of nodes, i and j), which is partially impacted by the control plane latency given in the following equation (assuming the incoming packet cannot be matched by flow rules in the respective switch).

$$L_{prop}^{n_i} + \sum_{k=1}^{w+1} L_{trans}^m + \sum_{k=1}^{w} (L_{queue}^m + L_{proc}^m) + Ctrl_{i,j}, \tag{1}$$

where $L_{prop}^{n_i}$ is the propagation delay at host n_i, L_{trans}^m is the transmission delay at the mth link, L_{queue}^m is the queuing delay at the mth switch, and L_{proc}^m

is the processing delay at the mth switch. Moreover, $ctrl_{i,j}$ is the delay of the control path due to the switch-controller communication (i.e., flow rule querying and insertion). Based on (1), the data-control channel latency can be induced by subtracting the respective measured delays from the overall end-to-end delay as it will be shown in Sect. 4.

Lastly, it is essential to note that the OpenFlow software version 1.5 (used in this work) standard offers several QoS capabilities and actions [2]. Specifically, the $set - queue$ features can associate a given queue ID for data flows, which can then be forwarded to further ports based upon a specific output function. Based upon the queue ID, we can decide which queue is attached to which port to schedule and or forward the data flow. However, these integral QoS-enabled queueing mechanisms and actions only provide basic QoS support, and thus further enhancements and implementations remain of substantial consideration. Therefore, in this work, we build upon the basic integral QoS capabilities in OpenFlow software to implement more complex QoS policing functions to classify data flows in multiple queue categories (while prioritizing control flows).

3.2   Latency Collection

The per-link latency is calculated based upon timestamps injections by the SDN controller via the Link Layer Discovery Protocol (LLDP) packets. Specifically, the SDN controller transmits these LLDP packets (i.e., as packet-outs) to all enabled switches in the network. Once the controller receives one of its transmitted LLDPs, it processes it as a Packet_In. Building upon this, the controller examines the LLDP packet timestamp and subtracts it from its current time (i.e., this computation gives the elapsed time). Lastly, the per-link latency will be the computation result of the elapsed time minus the latencies associated with switch-to-controller for the origin switch and the one that sent the Packet_In. For simplicity, the LLDP-based latency computation in our framework is induced as follows.

$$t\_lldp\_tx - t\_lldp\_rx - lat\_tx\_ovs - lat\_rx\_ovs \qquad (2)$$

where t_lldp_tx, t_lldp_rx, lat_tx_ovs, and lat_rx_ovs present the initial timestamp of the LLDP packet, the round trip time, latency in a neighboring switch that first receives and sends out the LLDP packet to the next switch, and latency in next-hop switch, respectively.

3.3   Latency Estimation

To minimize the controller's overhead caused by statistics collection, we implement an exponentially weighted moving average (EWMA) model for the short-run per-link latency metric estimation. This module uses per-link latencies calculated by the previous module (discussed in Subsect. 3.2), and obtain a new estimation of accumulated per-link latencies for an initialized window size that must be set by the network operator before launching the framework (10 sec. by default).

3.4   Path Selection

Inspired by the $A*$ algorithm [9], we implement a search heuristic $h(n)$ (where n is the source node) in the path selection module for the heuristic search of the optimal path from a source to a target node. Our path selection module only utilizes readily acquired per-link latency metric estimations (i.e., outputs of the latency estimation module described in Subsect. 3.3) between a particular communicating pair of nodes (source and target). The heuristic $h(n)$ is regarded as a set of paths between two communicating nodes, where the path cost is an estimate rather than an actual. In our path selector module implementation, we maintain two lists, $OPEN$ and $CLOSED$, for the list of pending paths (i.e., entities that are already visited but not expanded, and thus their successors are not checked yet). The list of entities that have been checked/expanded, and their successor nodes have been identified and put in the $OPEN$ list, respectively.

Building upon this, once the path estimates are obtained from the previous module, the path selection module uses them to compute the optimal path with minimal end-to-end latency. We select only the best two paths for overhead minimization if there are multiple paths between source and target nodes.

3.5   Queue Control and Control Flows Prioritization

In order for us to control the queue length and avert congestion, a minimum and maximum thresholds are defined and used for maintaining the average queue size at a midway (i.e., assuming the level of network congestion is medium). Furthermore, the proposed queue control mechanism averts dropping high priority packets. This aversion is achieved through the real-time computation of average queue size per data plane queue. The queue averages are updated based upon the controller feedback control message, i.e., if one or more data plane queues are congested, the forwarding device (OVS) is instructed to drop lower priority packets. Finally, to assure control packets are properly prioritized over data flows, the OpenFlow *Pause* action/message is leveraged. According to its flow table, the OVS can pause a packet's forwarding procedure while serializing the current packet state as *continuation* in the *Packet_In* message). Later on, the controller transmits a continuation flag back to the OVS using NXT_RESUME action, i.e., to resume flow processing from its previous interruption point.

4   Evaluation

In this section, we discuss the construction of our experimental topology on the Global Environment for Network Innovations (GENI), hardware and software setups, and experimental findings for our proposed framework's performance.

4.1   GENI Topology

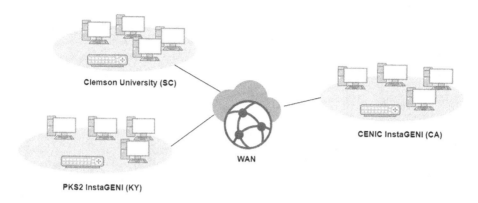

Fig. 3. Stitching multiple sites through GENI testbed for inter-region communications. The wide-area communication at scale is not restricted to one geographical site. GENI testbed allows inter-network domains for inter-region communications to support the elaboration of real-world experiments over the public Internet.

As the at-scale wide-area communication is not limited to one geographical region, GENI testbed grants inter network domains for inter-region communication in order to assist with elaborating real-world experiments over public Internet traffic. Thus, to better evaluate our framework's efficiency and evaluate the end-to-end delay within a topology connecting multiple sites, we deployed networking resources from multiple sites through the stitching capability of GENI, specifically, CA, KY, and SC as shown in Fig. 3. The constructed topology is depicted in Fig. 4. The GENI testbed's stitching capability allows for connecting nodes provided by multiple aggregates into a coherent real-world network.

4.2   Resource Setup

In order for us to conduct a realistic evaluation of the proposed SDN framework, the constructed networking topology must consist of the following.

1. SDN switching and routing devices
2. Software module to emulate networking traffic
3. Multiple paths and links with changeable throughput and packet loss

Additionally, open-source SDN controller and OpenFlow software implementations are chosen to ensure broader adoption/evaluation of the work. Next, realistic network traffic emulation is done using a dedicated software module. Finally, the network topology is designed with multiple paths and physical links with changeable loss rates and link speeds. As noted earlier, the solution is implemented in the NSF GENI network. This well-established testbed allows

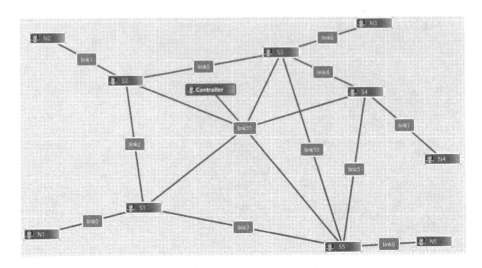

Fig. 4. A Constructed topology on GENI testbed, where multiple geographical locations (sites) are inter-connected through the stitching capabilities of GENI

researchers to build arbitrary network topology slices and deploy tailored end hosts (traffic generation) and SDN controllers.

Specifically, networking communications in these experiments are performed using mainly two tools, iPerf and hping3, as normal and burst traffic, respectively. Additionally, our at-scale topology's architectural design utilizes Open vSwitch (OVS) that supports OpenFlow software 1.5 along with Floodlight 1.2 as an SDN controller software, where the data plane queue (switching queue) is initially configured as follows.

```
$ ovs−vsctl add−br s0
$ ovs−vsctl add−port s0 eth0
$ ovs−vsctl set port eth0
qos=@newqos −− −−id=@newqos create qos
type=linux−htb
other−config:max−rate=5000000
queues:0=@newqueue −−
−−id=@newqueue create queue
other−config:min−rate=3000000
other−config:max−rate=3000000
```

4.3   Performance Results

The reported experimental runs are conducted for 15 successive trials in an automated manner, and the results are then averaged. Detailed results are now presented for % improvement of end-to-end delay, comparisons of end-to-end delay, and data-to-control latency between our framework and the default SDN controller software.

Table 1. % improvement of end-to-end delay in our framework with contrast to the default SDN Floodlight.

Statistic	Node N_1	Node N_2	Node N_3
Mean	6.02%	8.14%	9.38%
Median	6.76%	9.73%	8.92%

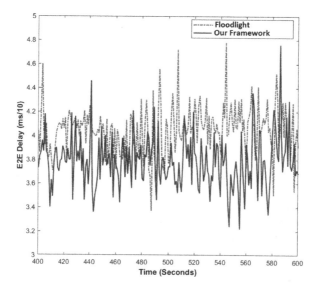

Fig. 5. A comparison of end-to-end delay between our framework and the default Floodlight SDN controller

Foremost, Our evaluation findings demonstrated that our developed framework outperforms the default optimization configurations in Floodlight SDN controller software. Table 1 and Fig. 5 give a summary of our comprehensive experiments. Specifically, Table 1 gives % end-to-end delay improvement in our framework, while Fig. 5 depicts a visual presentation of the delay in an end-to-end communication between designated nodes in our topology. In these experiments, we point N_1 and N_6 as a source node and a destination node, respectively. Figure 5 demonstrates our system outperforms the path selection mechanism adopted by Floodlight, and implies smaller end-to-end traffic delay. Table 1 shows that the proposed solution improves the average end-to-end delay by about 10%. This delay percentage is vital when delay-sensitive applications (e.g., emergency response systems) are built upon networked systems.

In this experiment, we aim at examining the efficiency of our solution in terms of control plane latency optimization between the same pair of switches in our GENI topology. Herein, the experiments take place on the same path between the switching devices. Moreover, it is important to state that we introduce additional networking traffic using the iPerf tool to simulate and perform link congestion at

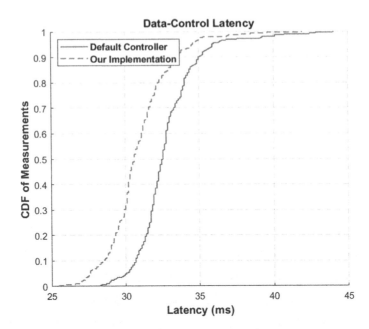

Fig. 6. A comparison of data-to-control latency in our framework vs. the one provided by the default Floodlight SDN controller software with a burst of traffic.

the intermediate switch on the path by adjusting the traffic burst. Specifically, we communicate 200 Mbps iPerf traffic shaping in this experimental scenario. We run both our framework and the non-optimized SDN controller (default Floodlight controller software) separately for five minutes.

Based on (1), we can induce the data-control channel latency by subtracting the respective measured delays from the overall end-to-end delay. Figure 6 presents the cumulative distribution functions (CDFs) of control-data plane latencies provided by our framework and default Floodlight SDN controller. As shown in Fig. 6, our queueing scheme outperforms the default controller with regard to control plane latency optimization.

5   Conclusions

In this paper, we presented a new SDN controller framework that enhances end-to-end QoS awareness. The proposed system utilizes various traffic engineering (TE) techniques, a queueing mechanism, real-time latency estimation, and heuristic path search to optimize the end-to-end latency in traffic delivery. The system enables prioritization of control plane traffic while minimizing the control plane latency through a priority queueing scheme. Our comprehensive experimentation was carried out over a continent-scale stitched topology (over multiple sites) built on the Global Environment for Network Innovations (GENI), a heterogeneous real-world testbed to experimentally evaluate the efficiency of the proposed framework. In the future work, we plan to integrate this framework into multi-domain SDN environment and explore other QoS metrics such as classification of networking traffic of varying priority levels and flow routing and forwarding with respect to the identified priorities.

Acknowledgment. We would like to acknowledge the National Science Foundation (NSF) that partially sponsored the work under grants #1633978, #1620871, #1620862, #1651280, #1531099 and BBN/GPO project #1936 through NSF/CNS grant. The views and conclusions contained herein are those of the authors and should not be interpreted as necessarily representing the official policies, either expressed or implied of NSF.

References

1. Floodlight openflow controller project. http://www.projectfloodlight.org/floodlight/
2. Openflow switch specification, version 1.5.1 (protocol version 0x06). https://www.opennetworking.org/wp-content/uploads/2014/10/openflow-switch-v1.5.1.pdf
3. Agarwal, S., Kodialam, M., Lakshman, T.: Traffic engineering in software defined networks. In: International Conference on Computer Communications, pp. 2211–2219. IEEE (2013)
4. Celenlioglu, M.R., Mantar, H.A.: An SDN based intra-domain routing and resource management model. In: International Conference on Cloud Engineering, pp. 347–352. IEEE (2015)
5. Chin, T., Rahouti, M., Xiong, K.: Applying software-defined networking to minimize the end-to-end delay of network services. ACM SIGAPP Appl. Comput. Rev. **18**(1), 30–40 (2018)
6. Chin, T., Xiong, K., Rahouti, M.: SDN-based kernel modular countermeasure for intrusion detection. In: Lin, X., Ghorbani, A., Ren, K., Zhu, S., Zhang, A. (eds.) SecureComm 2017. LNICST, vol. 238, pp. 270–290. Springer, Cham (2018). https://doi.org/10.1007/978-3-319-78813-5_14
7. Curtis, A.R., Mogul, J.C., Tourrilhes, J., Yalagandula, P., Sharma, P., Banerjee, S.: DevoFlow: scaling flow management for high-performance networks. In: SIG-COMM Computer Communication Review, vol. 41, pp. 254–265. ACM (2011)
8. Egilmez, H.E., Dane, S.T., Bagci, K.T., Tekalp, A.M.: OpenQoS: an openflow controller design for multimedia delivery with end-to-end quality of service over software-defined networks. In: Asia Pacific Signal and Information Processing Association Annual Summit and Conference, pp. 1–8. IEEE (2012)
9. Hart, P., Nilsson, N., Raphael, B.: A formal basis for the heuristic determination of minimum cost paths. IEEE Trans. Syst. Sci. Cybern. **4**(2), 100–107 (1968). https://doi.org/10.1109/tssc.1968.300136
10. Huang, D.Y., Yocum, K., Snoeren, A.C.: High-fidelity switch models for software-defined network emulation. In: SIGCOMM Workshop on Hot Topics in Software Defined Networking, pp. 43–48. ACM (2013)
11. Hussain, S.A., Akbar, S., Raza, I.: A dynamic multipath scheduling protocol (DMSP) for full performance isolation of links in software defined networking (SDN). In: Workshop on Recent Trends in Telecommunications Research, pp. 1–5. IEEE (2017)

12. Jain, S., et al.: B4: experience with a globally-deployed software defined WAN. In: SIGCOMM Computer Communication Review, vol. 43, pp. 3–14. ACM (2013)
13. Jarschel, M., Wamser, F., Hohn, T., Zinner, T., Tran-Gia, P.: SDN-based application-aware networking on the example of Youtube video streaming. In: European Workshop on Software Defined Networks, pp. 87–92. IEEE (2013)
14. McKeown, N., et al.: OpenFlow: enabling innovation in campus networks. ACM SIGCOMM Comput. Commun. Rev. **38**(2), 69–74 (2008)
15. Ni, H., Rahouti, M., Chakrabortty, A., Xiong, K., Xin, Y.: A distributed cloud-based wide-area controller with SDN-enabled delay optimization. In: Power & Energy Society General Meeting, pp. 1–5. IEEE (2018)
16. Rahouti, M., Xiong, K., Chin, T., Hu, P.: SDN-ERS: a timely software defined networking framework for emergency response systems. In: International Science of Smart City Operations and Platforms Engineering in Partnership with Global City Teams Challenge, pp. 18–23. IEEE (2018)
17. Rahouti, M., Xiong, K., Chin, T., Hu, P., De Oliveira, D.: A preemption-based timely software defined networking framework for emergency response traffic delivery. In: International Conference on High Performance Computing and Communications; International Conference on Smart City; International Conference on Data Science and Systems, pp. 452–459. IEEE (2019)
18. Rahouti, M., Xiong, K., Xin, Y., Ghani, N.: Latencysmasher: a software-defined networking-based framework for end-to-end latency optimization. In: 2019 IEEE 44th Conference on Local Computer Networks, pp. 202–209. IEEE (2019)
19. Rotsos, C., Sarrar, N., Uhlig, S., Sherwood, R., Moore, A.W.: OFLOPS: an open framework for OpenFlow switch evaluation. In: Taft, N., Ricciato, F. (eds.) PAM 2012. LNCS, vol. 7192, pp. 85–95. Springer, Heidelberg (2012). https://doi.org/10.1007/978-3-642-28537-0_9
20. Sharma, S., et al.: Implementing quality of service for the software defined networking enabled future Internet. In: The European Workshop on Software Defined Networking, pp. 49–54. IEEE (2014)
21. Tariq, S., Bassiouni, M.: QAMO-SDN: QoS aware multipath TCP for software defined optical networks. In: Annual Consumer Communications and Networking Conference, pp. 485–491. IEEE (2015)
22. Yan, J., Zhang, H., Shuai, Q., Liu, B., Guo, X.: HiQoS: an SDN-based multipath QoS solution. China Commun. **12**(5), 123–133 (2015)
23. Yu, T.F., Wang, K., Hsu, Y.H.: Adaptive routing for video streaming with QoS support over SDN networks. In: International Conference on Information Networking, pp. 318–323. IEEE (2015)
24. Zhang, T., Liu, B.: Exposing end-to-end delay in software-defined networking. Int. J. Reconfig. Comput. **2019** (2019)

Precision Improvement of Overprinting System Based on Improved Laplace Edge Detection Algorithm

Yingbo Wang[✉], Likun Lu, Qingtao Zeng, Rui Zhao, Yang Zhang, and Fucheng You

Beijing Institute of Graphic Communication, Beijing, People's Republic of China

Abstract. This paper proposes a solution to locate the crossline center in overprinting system. Crosslines of 4 different colors are printed at the same coordinate. Because of mechanical error, they do not coincide. The system uses the measured deviation to calibrate. This paper obtains accurate deviation value through three steps. First, the picture collected by a CCD camera will be processed by color segregation algorithm. In this process, RGB data turn into CMYK data, and each color will be on a single picture. After that, a Laplace edge detection algorithm is improved by combining it with 2D Gauss filter. This improved Laplace edge detection algorithm has a better noise suppression effect, which means it is even less likely to judge noise as the edge of a graph. Finally, target searching algorithm based on rhombus matching is used to figure out the center of crossline. The average absolute error from 2,000 simulations is 3.192 pixel, which shows that the algorithm in this paper has a high accuracy.

Keywords: Laplace edge detection · Overprint · Color segment · Crossline

1 Introduction

Overprinting is an important method of color printing [1]. The basic principle of overprinting is that several different colors of ink are printed to the same paper in sequence [2]. When all the different colors are painted, all the print heads need the same frame of reference. It requires a high location precision, or the final prints will be misplaced.

Today, overprinting system is running at a relatively higher speed, which leads to a lower printing precision. To make sure the printing precision meets the requirements, we must limit the printing speed. At the same time, how to evaluate the quality of the prints effectively is also an important task. If we do not find out and solve the problems of printing precision in time, a waste of time and money will not be avoided resulting from defective prints, especially in industrial production.

The paper aims at solving the above problems. First the color picture is divided into four color channels [3–5]: C, M, Y and K. After that we use improved Laplace edge detection algorithm to locate the center of the crossline. Then the deviations of channel K to channel C, M and Y are calculated. And the deviation is the overprinting error. This paper makes the overprinting error more accurate. As a result, the whole overprinting system can work more accurately. And the printing quality can also be improved.

Y. Weng et al. (Eds.): TridentCom 2020, LNICST 380, pp. 17–26, 2021.
https://doi.org/10.1007/978-3-030-77428-8_2

2 Traditional Crossline Detection Methods

Crossline detection is important in many industries. To make every color print head work accurately, we often need to print a crossline of each color and locate the crossline center by a photo token by a high-speed CCD camera [6], to realize the calibration of overprinting system. If we can get a clear photo of the crossline, the method is pretty good.

However, the photos usually are of a low signal-to-noise ratio and contrast. There are often some limitations in traditional crossline detection methods, such as Hough transform [7], template matching [8], morphological corrosion [9], linear fitting and so on.

The result using linear fitting will be of a large deviation if the edge of a crossline image is irregular [10, 11]. And the result using morphological corrosion will not find the crossline center precisely if the contrast of the photo is not high enough.

3 Error Detection Based on Overlay Quasi-identifier

3.1 Overprinting Quality Detection Method

Traditionally, the overprinting error detection process is realized by examining the overlay quasi-identifier artificially. Figure 1 shows three kinds of different overlay quasi-identifiers.

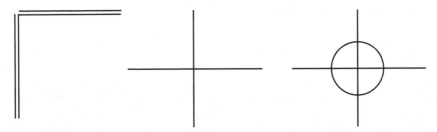

Fig. 1. Common overprint overlay quasi-identifiers

If the deviation is larger than the line width, usually 1 mm, we support that the overprinting system is not working well. Also, the prints are off specification.

The crossline detection processing framework is shown as Fig. 2. First, a picture of the print is collected by an imaging sensor, for example, a CCD camera. And then four crosslines of C, M, Y and K purity colors can be processed by image segmentation.

Fig. 2. Crossline center locating processing framework

After that we locate the center of each crossline by image edge detection algorithm. We can judge whether the overprinting system is working exactly or not.

If the overprinting system is not working well, a calibration can be implemented.

3.2 Color Segmentation Method

A significant step of the detection using computer vision is how to get the data of channel C, M, Y and K. According to the relation of RGB and CMYK, there is not a one-to-one correspondence. If we transform RGB to CMYK, there must be a replacement value for the black color. The replacement value can be figured out by C, M and Y channel. In fact, RGB color range is 0–255, and CMYK color range is 0–100. So, we can get the transform relation as:

$$
\begin{bmatrix} c \\ m \\ y \end{bmatrix} = \begin{bmatrix} G_{max} \\ G_{max} \\ G_{max} \end{bmatrix} - \begin{bmatrix} R \\ G \\ B \end{bmatrix} \tag{1}
$$

$$
K = \min(c, m, y) \tag{2}
$$

$$
C = c - K \tag{3}
$$

$$
M = m - K \tag{4}
$$

$$
Y = y - K \tag{5}
$$

In the expressions, G_{max} is the most value of a color, and usually it is 255.

In actual situations, four different color crosslines may be in several kinds of states. The four crosslines can be separated from each other. And it can be that two crosslines are overlapped and another two is separated. Or three crosslines are overlapping. All in all, the overlapping relation is complicated.

Some scholars propose an approach to solve the problem. First, we need to judge which overlapping relation the crosslines are in. And for a certain relation, we use a different threshold to divide the picture. As we learned, there are 15 different color overlap, so we need 14 threshold values. This method requires a high color precision and how to judge which color relation the crosslines belonging to is difficult.

To solve this problem, we a method mentioned in reference. Figure 3 shows the flow of this method.

4 Improved Laplacian Edge Detection Algorithm

In the previous section, we discussed how to make overlapping crosslines separated from each other. In this section, we will solve the problem of how to find the crossline center by an improved Laplacian edge detection algorithm.

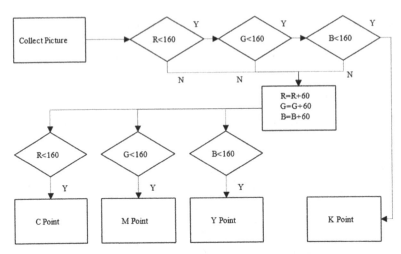

Fig. 3. color segmentation method flow chart

4.1 The Disadvantage of Laplacian Operator

The 2D-Laplace transform is based on 2D-gradient. And the definition is as follow.

$$
\begin{aligned}
\nabla^2 f(x, y) &= \frac{\partial^2 f(x, y)}{\partial^2 x} + \frac{\partial^2 f(x, y)}{\partial^2 x} \\
&\approx \frac{\partial[f(x+1, y) - f(x, y)]}{\partial x} + \frac{\partial[f(x, y+1) - f(x, y)]}{\partial y} \\
&\approx f(x+1, y) - f(x, y) - [f(x, y) - f(x-1, y)] \\
&\quad + f(x, y+1) - f(x, y) - [f(x, y) - f(x, y-1)] \\
&\approx f(x+1, y) + f(x-1, y) + f(x, y+1) + f(x, y-1) - 4f(x, y) \quad (6)
\end{aligned}
$$

2D-Laplace transform is usually expressed by a convolution of a matrix and a Laplace core. And we can get the following equations.

$$
I = \begin{pmatrix} 0 & -1 & 0 \\ -1 & 4 & -1 \\ 0 & -1 & 0 \end{pmatrix} \quad (7)
$$

$$
I_- = \begin{pmatrix} 0 & 1 & 0 \\ 1 & -4 & 1 \\ 0 & 1 & 0 \end{pmatrix} \quad (8)
$$

And the 2D-Laplace transform can be described as follow.

$$
\begin{cases} \nabla^2 f(x, y) = P * I \\ \nabla^2 f(x, y) = P * I_- \end{cases} \quad (9)
$$

In the above equations, * means convolution, and I is Laplace core.

These equations show that if we want to figure out the convolution result of picture matrix P and Laplace core I or I_-, actually we will figure out the difference value between the value of a certain pixel and the neighboring horizontal and vertical pixels. The convolution result is four times this difference.

Traditional Laplace edge detection uses the location of zero point or the convolution result to find out the edge of figures. This method may take noise point as an edge with high probability. It is because that Laplace operator is not of the feature of smoothing the picture, which is available for Sobel operator or Prewitt operator.

4.2 Improvement of Laplace Operator Using 2D-Gaussian Function

In this section we combine traditional Laplace edge detection with Gaussian function. 2D-Gaussian function is defined as:

$$\text{Gauss}(x, y, \sigma) = \frac{1}{2\pi\sigma^2} \exp\left(-\frac{x^2 + y^2}{2\sigma^2}\right) \tag{10}$$

Improved Laplacian edge detection based on Gaussian smoothing filter is as follow:

Step 1: Figure out Gaussian matrix $G_{H \times W}$ according to Eq. (10).

$$G_{H \times W} = \left[\text{Gauss}(x, y, \sigma)\right]_{0 \leq x \leq H-1, 0 \leq y \leq W-1, x, y \in N} \tag{11}$$

Step 2: Figure out the sum of Gaussian matrix.

$$sum = \sum G_{H \times W} \tag{12}$$

Step 3: Normalize. It means that the Gaussian matrix is divide by the sum. Then we get the Gaussian convolution operator K.

$$K = \frac{G_{H \times W}}{sum} \tag{13}$$

Step 4: The image matrix P is convolved with the Gaussian convolution operator K. After the Gaussian smoothing filter, the result will be convolved with Laplace core I or I_-.

$$\begin{cases} R_{\text{conv}} = P * K * I \\ R_{\text{conv}} = P * K * I_- \end{cases} \tag{14}$$

4.3 Algorithm Optimization

The time complexity of the algorithm in Sect. 3.2 is high, because it requires 2D convolution. We can optimize the algorithm by turning the 2D convolution into 1D convolutions. The process is as follows.

Step 1: Take the Laplace transform of 2D-Gaussian function.

$$\nabla^2\big[\text{Gauss}(x, y, \sigma)\big] = \frac{\nabla^2\big[\text{Gauss}(x, y, \sigma)\big]}{\partial^2 x} + \frac{\nabla^2\big[\text{Gauss}(x, y, \sigma)\big]}{\partial^2 y}$$

$$= \frac{1}{2\pi\sigma^2}\left[\begin{array}{c} \dfrac{\partial\left(-\frac{x}{\sigma^2}\exp\left(-\frac{x^2+y^2}{2\sigma^2}\right)\right)}{\partial x} \\[2mm] +\dfrac{\partial\left(-\frac{y}{\sigma^2}\exp\left(-\frac{x^2+y^2}{2\sigma^2}\right)\right)}{\partial y} \end{array}\right]$$

$$= \frac{1}{2\pi\sigma^4}\left(\frac{x^2}{\sigma^2} - 1\right)\exp\left(-\frac{x^2+y^2}{2\sigma^2}\right)$$

$$+ \frac{1}{2\pi\sigma^4}\left(\frac{y^2}{\sigma^2} - 1\right)\exp\left(-\frac{x^2+y^2}{2\sigma^2}\right)$$

$$= \frac{1}{2\pi\sigma^4}\left(\frac{x^2+y^2}{2\sigma^2} - 2\right)\exp\left(-\frac{x^2+y^2}{2\sigma^2}\right) \qquad (15)$$

Step 2: Construct an operator K^I, whose window size is $H \times W$, and the standard deviation is σ

$$K^I = \nabla^2\left(\text{Gauss}\left(x - \frac{H-1}{2}, y - \frac{W-1}{2}, \sigma\right)\right)$$

$$0 \le x \le H, 0 \le y \le W \qquad (16)$$

Step 3: Convolve picture matrix P and improved Laplace operator K^I, then we can get $R_{\text{conv}} = P * K^I$. Use R_{conv} to resolve Eq. (15).

$$\nabla^2(\text{Gauss}(x, y, \sigma)) = \frac{1}{2\pi\sigma^4}\left(\frac{x^2+y^2}{2\sigma^2} - 2\right)\cdot\exp\left(-\frac{x^2+y^2}{2\sigma^2}\right)$$

$$= \left(\frac{x^2+y^2}{\sigma^2} - 2\right)\cdot\frac{\text{Gauss}(x, \sigma)\cdot\text{Gauss}(y, \sigma)}{\sigma^2} \qquad (17)$$

$$\text{Gauss}(x, \sigma) = \frac{1}{\sigma\sqrt{2\pi}}\exp\left(-\frac{x^2}{2\sigma^2}\right) \qquad (18)$$

$$\text{Gauss}(y, \sigma) = \frac{1}{\sigma\sqrt{2\pi}}\exp\left(-\frac{y^2}{2\sigma^2}\right) \qquad (19)$$

Step 4: Binarization process. And the edge detection result can be worked out.

$$edge(x, y) = \begin{cases} 255, & R_{\text{conv}} > 0 \\ 0, & R_{\text{conv}} \le 0 \end{cases} \qquad (20)$$

Or:

$$edge(x, y) = \begin{cases} 255, & R_{\text{conv}} < 0 \\ 0, & R_{\text{conv}} \geq 0 \end{cases} \tag{21}$$

In step 3, the 2D-covnlution is turned into 1D-convlution, which leads to a lower time complexity. In step 4, not like Prewitt operator or Sobel operator, we do not take the absolute value of R_{conv}. Instead, Eq. (20) or (21) is used to judge the probability of if a pixel is the edge or not.

5 Determine the Center Coordinates of the Crosslines

In Sects. 3.1, 3.2 and 3.3, we get the edge of the crosslines. In this section the center coordinates will be determined by a target searching algorithm.

5.1 Target Searching Algorithm Based on Rhombus Matching

First, we define $S_{i,j}$ as the pixel value of each color crosslines. $S_{i,j} = 1$ when a pixel belongs to a certain color (C, M, Y or K), or $S_{i,j} = 0$. Figure 4 shows the rhombus matching template.

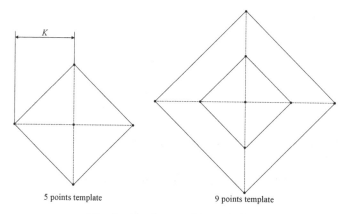

5 points template   9 points template

Fig. 4. rhombus matching template

In Fig. 4, K is related to the size of crosslines. It is the horizontal or vertical distance between neighbor points. And in the following searching process, step-size is L. Take $K = 9$ for example.

Step 1: If a pixel point (m, n) is on the crossline, which means that it satisfies $S_{m,n} = 1$, then 3×3 template is used. And go to step 2. If not, go to step 4.

Step 2: If there are 5 points on the crossline, we use 5×5 template. And go to step 3. If not, go to step 4.

Step 3: If there 9 points on the crossline, this point (m, n) is the center of the crossline. If not, go to step 4.

Step 4: Update the pixel point with the following equations. Do step 1–4 again, until it meets the reequipments.

$$(m, n)' = (m + L, n) \tag{22}$$

$$(m, n)' = (m, n + L) \tag{23}$$

5.2 Additional Cases for Practical Application

The line width is usually more than one pixel. As a result, the center point may be more than one, for a certain color. Then we just need to figure out the average of these center points as the center of crosslines.

Define x and y as the center point (x, y), we can get:

$$x = \frac{1}{N} \sum_{i=1}^{N} m_i \tag{24}$$

$$y = \frac{1}{N} \sum_{i=1}^{N} n_i \tag{25}$$

In the equations, N is the total number of center points before averaging.

6 Precision Improvement of Overprinting System

Based on the center point of crosslines of different colors, we can figure out the error of the overprinting system. If the location of the four centers is at the same point, the printing system is working well. If it is not the same, we need to calibrate the reference frame of the nozzles. In fact, this process is performed by computer.

7 Simulation and Experimental Results Analysis

In this paper, we use MATLAB to process image data and all the algorithm is implemented. In this section, the results are showed out.

We use MATLAB to process the collected images. For example, Fig. 5(a) shows an actual picture printed by a certain model of overprinting system.

Figure 5(b)–(e) shows C, M, Y and K grayscale images after the color segmentation. From the images we can see that the main feature of each different color channel is extracted reasonably.

After the color segmentation, we judge the center coordinate of every crossline. We use the simulation program to randomly generate some crosslines with known central coordinates. The method in this paper is used to calculate the central coordinates of the

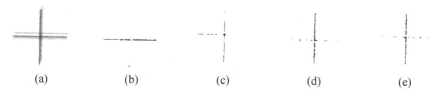

(a)   (b)   (c)   (d)   (e)

Fig. 5. Color segmentation result

crosslines. And then we calculate the absolute error between the real value and the value calculated by the algorithm.

$$\varepsilon = \sqrt{(x - x_0)^2 + (y - y_0)^2} \qquad (26)$$

In Eq. (26), x and y mean the value calculated by the algorithm. x_0 and y_0 are the real values. Table 1 shows some results of the simulation experiment. The unit in the table is pixel. All pictures are 256 * 256.

Table 1. Simulation results of improved Laplace algorithm

No.	x	y	x_0	y_0	ε
1	132	106	133.71	102.71	3.706
2	120	144	120.00	143.71	0.286
3	149	113	151.57	109.86	4.061
4	160	111	163.57	111.00	3.571
5	85	141	83.14	140.29	1.990
6	166	122	170.14	126.29	5.961
7	163	154	165.57	156.71	3.739
8	87	132	83.14	132.86	3.951
9	167	125	171.29	125.43	4.307
10	165	133	163.29	137.14	4.484

The average absolute error from 2,000 simulations is 3.192 pixel. This shows that the algorithm in this paper has a high positioning accuracy.

8 Summary and Prospect

This paper improved the edge detection algorithm in overprinting calibration. According to the results in experiment, the algorithm in this paper is of a higher precision. Using this method can improve the quality of color printing.

However, compared with traditional methods, this algorithm requires more matrix operations. This is not conducive to real-time monitoring at printing time. One possible solution is to make use of GPU or FPGA to speed up the process. And this is a further study issue.

Acknowledgements. This publication is based on work supported in part by major special project of science and technology of Guangdong Province, No. 190826175545233 and Beijing science and technology innovation service capability construction project, No. PXM2016_014223_000025, and BIGC Project (Ec202007). Any opinions, findings and conclusions or recommendations expressed in this publication are those of the authors and do not necessarily reflect the views of the funding agency.

References

1. Jia, W.: A novel image registration control system based on improved composite metric entropy function in color printing. Multimed. Tools Appl. **79**, 9225–9236 (2020)
2. Seipel, S., Yu, J., Viková, M., et al.: Color performance, durability and handle of inkjet-printed and UV-cured photochromic textiles for multi-colored applications. Fibers Polym. **20**, 1424–1435 (2019)
3. Chen, X., Wang, Q., Lee, Y.: Real-time demosaicking method based on mixed color channel correlation. J. Real-Time Image Proc. **16**, 61–69 (2019)
4. Darwish, S.M., Al-Khafaji, L.D.S.: Dual watermarking for color images: a new image copyright protection model based on the fusion of successive and segmented watermarking. Multimed. Tools Appl. **79**, 6503–6530 (2020)
5. Hinojosa, S., Oliva, D., Cuevas, E., et al.: Reducing overlapped pixels: a multi-objective color thresholding approach. Soft. Comput. **24**, 6787–6807 (2020)
6. Baldi, A.: Digital image correlation and color cameras. Exp. Mech. **58**, 315–333 (2018)
7. Yang, C., Collins, J.: Improvement of honey bee tracking on 2D video with hough transform and Kalman filter. J. Sig. Process. Syst. **90**, 1639–1650 (2018)
8. Chen, F., Ye, X., Yin, S., et al.: Automated vision positioning system for dicing semiconductor chips using improved template matching method. Int. J. Adv. Manuf. Technol. **100**, 2669–2678 (2019)
9. Cao, X., Gao, S., Chen, L., et al.: Ship recognition method combined with image segmentation and deep learning feature extraction in video surveillance. Multimed. Tools Appl. **79**, 9177–9192 (2020)
10. Bi, Q., Huang, J., Lu, Y., et al.: A general, fast and robust B-spline fitting scheme for micro-line tool path under chord error constraint. Sci. China Technol. Sci. **62**, 321–332 (2019)
11. Maity, R.: Regression analysis and curve fitting. Statistical Methods in Hydrology and Hydroclimatology. STCEE, pp. 229–257. Springer, Singapore (2018). https://doi.org/10.1007/978-981-10-8779-0_7

Requirements for Deploying IP and ICN Network Stacks on a Common Physical Infrastructure

Renan Krishna[1]([✉])[iD] and Roger Baig Vinas[2][iD]

[1] Interdigital Europe, London, UK
renan.krishna@interdigital.com
[2] Universitat Politècnica de Catalunya, Barcelona, Catalunya, Spain
rbaig@ac.upc.edu
https://www.interdigital.com/, https://dsg.ac.upc.edu/

Abstract. Deploying alternative networks such as Information Centric Network (ICN) in a production/commercial network with real users is challenging due to the experimental nature of these novel proposals. To meet these challenges, we adopted an ICN-IP dual stack approach. However, this was at the cost of introducing unpredictable emergent behavior. This behavior can be dealt with by a set of requirements presented in this paper. These requirements specify a constraining discipline on the deployment and operational processes for the dual stack making such processes tractable. The requirements are extracted from our experience of a lab deployment followed by a field deployment with real users as part of the three-year long EU-funded architectuRe for an Internet For Every-body (RIFE) project. We summarize them in a form that can be used by other practitioners in their own ICN/alternative network stack deployments and by tool developers for such deployments. These presented requirements compliment the current discussions within the Centric Networking Research Group (ICNRG) of the Internet Research Task Force (IRTF).

Keywords: Information-Centric Networking · Deployment · Testbed · Requirements · Tools

1 Introduction

It has been recently articulated that there are three distinct levels for the process of designing an Inter-network [23]. At the highest level are the core principles as well as basic design decisions of the architecture. Next level is the design

This work received financial support through the European Union H2020 Research and Innovation Programme, Grant Agreement No 644663, by the Spanish State Research Agency (AEI) under contracts PCI2019-111850-2 and PCI2019-111851-2 grants, and by the Spanish Ministry of Science and Innovation under contract PID2019-106774RB-C21.

of mechanisms that convert the architecture into an implementation. Finally, at the lowest level are the set of decisions about deployment that result in an operational Inter-network.

To design an Internetwork, the Information Centric Network (ICN) architecture has emerged as one of the many new paradigms. There have been several proposals for an Information Centric Network architecture over the past few years [1–6, 8, 10–12, 19–21]. A recent Internet-Draft [22] by the Information-Centric Networking Research Group (ICNRG) of the Internet Research Task Force (IRTF) has discussed several deployment considerations for a live deployment of the ICN architecture thereby contributing to the discussions at the lowest level of the abstraction hierarchy of [23].

In this paper, we elaborate on the lessons learnt in the field trial of the project called architectuRe for an Internet For Everybody (RIFE) [9] mentioned in that draft [22] and which is at the lowest level of the aforementioned hierarchy of [23]. In particular, we discuss RIFE's dual IP-ICN deployment which allowed us to alternate between either of them as an underlay [22] while providing Internet services to real users in the field. This paper thus compliments the discussion in that Internet-Draft.

The challenge in the field trial was to deal with problems that emerge within a tight time schedule when setting up two different OSI network layers on the same physical network. Such a setup faces the problem of having to run ICN software over an infrastructure that is optimized for the IP world. Moreover, the two network layers sharing common machines interact with each other in a manner that results in an unpredictable emergent behavior. To deal with such problems, an appropriate workflow needs to be developed to coordinate the activities of the ICN deployer and the network operator. Additionally, an easy way to switch traffic from ICN back to IP is required to deal with bugs in the ICN code and ensure that the users can still access an operational network.

We present a set of general requirements that can be followed by practitioners seeking to deploy an alternative network architecture on an operational infrastructure with real users. In addition, these requirements can guide the development of tools for such deployments. In particular, our contributions are:

– We describe a way to impose a common vocabulary through code for the naming, the order of initialization and error specification of hardware/software components that should be used both by the network operator and the ICN deployer. We discuss why this is important for dealing with unpredictable emergent behavior resulting from the way the two network stacks interact with each other on common machines (Sect. 4).
– We describe a way to achieve a switch between the IP and ICN networks such that the user's experience is not disrupted and at the same time is easy and convenient for the network operator. We discuss why this is important in field-trial deployments (Sect. 4).
– We have produced a set of requirements that provide constraining guidelines to instantiate the configuration of the IP and ICN software on the production networks whilst respecting the precedence constraints on the compo-

nents of the network. These requirements are general enough to be useful for Inter-network layers other than ICN and for development of tools for such deployments (Sect. 5).

The rest of this paper is structured as follows: In Sect. 2, we give an overview of the ICN flavor that we deployed, Sect. 3 explains in details the problems that we faced when deploying our ICN implementation in the operator's network, Sect. 4 describes how we solved those problems, Sect. 5 summarizes the lessons we learnt from our deployment into a set of requirements, Sect. 6 discusses the related work, and finally in Sect. 7 we present our conclusions.

2   A Brief Overview of ICN

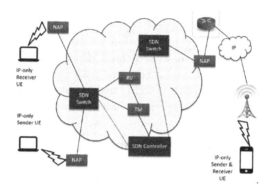

Fig. 1. ICN architecture.

The system architecture used by the RIFE project (Fig. 1) aims to replace the network of an individual network operator, so as to improve the IP-based services that it offers to its customers [3]. RIFE does not require any changes to the existing IP User Equipment (UE) connecting to the operator's network, or to the IP routers/gateways of other interconnected operators. This is achieved by combining an ICN, which forms the core of the RIFE network, with a set of Network Attachment Points (NAPs), which reside at the periphery of the RIFE network, serving as gateways between the IP and ICN worlds. The baseline architecture was derived from the Framework Programme 7 (FP7) Publish Subscribe Internet Technology (PURSUIT) ICN architecture, in which the end-user nodes can publish and subscribe to named information items. This publish/subscribe architecture implemented in a software called Blackadder is facilitated by three core functions: a Rendezvous (RV) function that matches publisher and subscriber nodes; a Topology Manager (TM) function that calculates paths between the various nodes and encodes them into Forwarding Identifiers (FIDs); and, a Forwarding Node function that allows data items to be forwarded in the network based on the FIDs. We now describe the NAP, Forwarder (FWD), RV and TM functions of the ICN architecture:

- Network Attachment Point: In order to preserve the IP interfaces towards UEs and other operators, RIFE uses a gateway approach. The NAPs, e.g. the access gateways of customers to the network, or the gateways of the network to peering networks or operator server resources, handle all the offered protocols at the IP interface, either directly as IP packets, or, if possible, as transport or application layer messages, for example, as HTTP messages. Thus, this NAP implementation allows us to use an IP-over- ICN abstraction in the Field Trial. See [7] for more details on how this is done. The NAP function can also be used as a GateWay (GW) to the Internet.
- Forwarder (FWD): A core function is that of delivering the information from the source(s) to the sink(s), i.e., the publisher(s) to the subscriber(s). Software Defined Networking (SDN) switches are used for the Forwarding (FWD) functionality.
- Rendezvous and Topology Manager: The RV maintains IP and Fully Qualified Domain Name (FQDN) subscription information that is then used to facilitate its matching function. When the TM receives a topology formation notification from the RV, it uses a shortest path calculation between a publisher and subscriber. This path is then encoded by OR-ing the FIDs (in the form of bit strings) and the result is included in each packet.

3   Dual Stack Deployment Problems

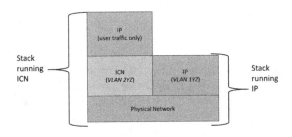

Fig. 2. The ICN and IP stacks.

Consider Fig. 2 where two stacks that we ran in parallel over the common physical network are shown. The ICN stack (left) was used to carry the users' traffic which as discussed in the previous section was only IP traffic although the same setting allows for other ICN traffic such as HTTP and Constrained Application Protocol (CoAP). Additionally, ICN signaling traffic was also carried over this stack.

The IP stack was used to carry the management traffic of the network operator and, optionally, the users' traffic. This user traffic could be switched by the operator to the IP from ICN stack and vice-versa. The IP stack was also used as a backup to access the ICN devices.

We now identify the following six problems that needed to be addressed to enable a successful deployment:

Problem 1. The deployment network architecture had to be designed to facilitate an error-free and easy to debug running of the ICN software. The deployment that followed this design had to include a suitable topology and a suitable configuration of the network infrastructure.

Problem 2. The ICN and the management IP networks needed to be isolated from each other using techniques that facilitated an error-free deployment. This isolation is required not only to prevent the two networks from interfering in each other's functioning but also to have an ability to identify the network from which a problem originates. Moreover, such an isolation enables a systematic allocation of resources such as ports, interfaces etc. and simplifies the initialization scripts.

Problem 3. We needed a way to deal with unpredictable emergent behavior during the initialization of the ICN network. This behavior emerges even when the ICN and the IP management networks are isolated (using VLAN) from each other because the two isolated network share physical resources and the VLAN scheme provides no means to fairly distribute bandwidth between them.

The emergent behavior is a consequence of the way the configuration of the two stacks interact with each other. Often, these behaviors are hard to predict prior to a deployment. Some examples of such emergent behavior that we had to face in our deployment include:

a) Loops involving broadcast/multicast MAC frames circulating in the various VLANs led to a complete network meltdown with SSH access becoming impossible. As a result, we were unable to even run our scripts to deploy the ICN network.
b) Low ICN throughput of 0.5 Mbps–1.5 Mbps rather than the expected value of around 20 Mbps with TCP traffic was observed.

Thus, we needed a way to deal with this non- deterministic behavior of the interaction between the operator's network providing IP-based management services and the ICN network. This behavior can emerge despite all the components of the ICN and IP-based networks individually showing deterministic behavior.

Besides the deployment challenges discussed above, following challenges were faced while running an ICN in the real world:

Problem 4. We needed to develop a workflow to coordinate between the network operator and the ICN deployer to deal with debugging problems that arose out of the unpredictable emergent behavior of running ICN. Often, the process to deal with this behavior can be tedious, time- consuming and error prone. In addition, the deployed equipment was a 100km drive away and a misdiagnosis of the causes for the errant behavior could result in a waste of time, effort and money.

Problem 5. The ICN network needed to be monitored to ensure that no component had crashed. To respond to a crash, coordination was required between the remote deployer (in London) of the ICN network and the local operator (in Barcelona) of the physical infrastructure. Similarly, the ICN network needed to be monitored for performance. To respond to performance issues, again coordination as described above was required.

Problem 6. We needed a way to ensure that the real-world users could have access to the internet even when the ICN network was stopped for debugging purposes.

4 Deployment Solution

We now discuss the solutions to the problems described in the previous section.

Solution to Problem 1. The field-trial was based on Wireless fielity (WiFi) technologies (for their ease of deployment) and deployed in the Guifi.net community network [24]. In this community network, the network infrastructure is heterogeneous (the project is defined to be technologically neutral) with WiFi and optical fiber being the most common technologies that have been used [25]. To keep our deployment simple, the ICN software that we used only supported static network topologies and at the physical network level we just used WiFi in infrastructure mode. The alternative to WiFi links were optical fiber links, but this option was discarded not only due to time and budget constraints, but also because challenging topologies are more difficult to achieve (fiber deployments are commonly much less meshed than WiFi deployments). The Ad-hoc WiFi mode was discarded due to the high variability of the link qualities and the high connectivity degree between nodes.

In infrastructure mode there are two different types of nodes (a node is a geographical location with network equipment): the Super Nodes (SNs) and the End-nodes (ENs). The nodes are connected to each other through links. Topologically speaking, the SNs are the nodes with more than one link to other nodes (i.e. they extend the network) while the ENs are just linked to one SN (i.e. they are the leaves in a graph). The links between SNs are point-to- point links, usually built with highly directive antennae, forming the backbone network. The links between ENs and their SN are usually point-to-multipoint links, built with sector antennae, also referred as Access Points (APs). The resulting topology is the same as that of the most common wired deployments.

Figure 3 shows a generic SN. In addition to the directive and sector antennae, its main components include: a core router, an (unmanaged) switch and a number

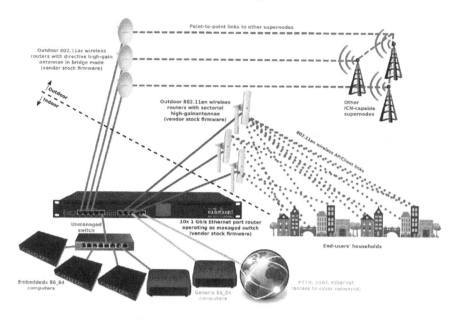

Fig. 3. Generic supernode architecture.

Table 1. Computing devices.

Name	Function
FWD	ICN FWD
NAP	ICN NAP
RVTM	ICN RVTM
SRV	Apache server
AUX	General purpose Linux box. Has one IP of each AP subnetwork
CLE	Linux box with LXC. Replaces an AP. Emulates the whole AP-end-user nodes construction
ALT	General purpose Linux box. Runs DHCP client in an interface. Aimed at reaching devices hidden behind a NAT

of ICN Computing Devices (CDs) described in Table 1, and so on. It also shows the interconnection links for transit or peering.

We deployed two experimental facilities- one was a production network with 40 end-users in several villages, and the other in a laboratory as a partial reproduction of the production network. In our implementations the core routers were connected to up to three directive antennae and up to three APs. In the laboratory's deployment, some APs and the attached Customer Premises Equipment (CPEs) were replaced by Client emulators (CLEs), Linux boxes which emulated sets of APs and the associated ENs.

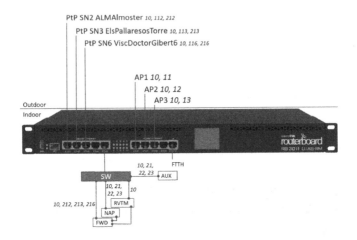

Fig. 4. SN1 router. Ports' assignment.

In our deployments the ICN functions NAP and FWD were each implemented by an independent CD to enable an easy isolation of problems such as software crashes, performance issues, misconfiguration of software/hardware etc. Figure 4 shows the ICN CDs wiring. The RV and TM functions are performed by another CD called RVTM. Note that there is one RVTM per deployment. Its first Ethernet port is attached to the switch and the second to the third port of the FWD. There is one NAP for each SN with ENs. Each SN has a forwarding function which is performed by the CD called FWD. The first Ethernet port of the NAP and the FWD is connected to the switch and the second port connects them to each other.

Solution to Problem 2. We isolated the two networks; the ICN network and the IP-based management network into separate VLANs.

We now discuss the VLAN naming conventions that we followed, how we configured the routers in the super nodes to support the VLANs, and how we organized the IP addresses to support our VLANs.

The VLANs were named so that they were semantically meaningful. For our deployments, this semantic structure was used to identify the network (IP, ICN) and the nodes and interfaces involved as described below:

- Each point-to-point link had two VLANs XYZ; X = 1 for the IP network, X = 2 for the ICN network; Y was the lower SN number; Z the higher SN number. The SNs were numbered from 1 to 6. For example, a point-to-point link between SN1 and SN6 will have two VLANs: VLAN 116 for the IP network and VLAN 216 for the ICN network.
- The FWD had the corresponding 2YZ VLANs (first Network Interface Controller (NIC)). For example, the FWD on SN1's point-to-point link to SN6 will have its first NIC connected to VLAN 216.

- The VLANs of the APs were 1A; A = 1 for AP1, A = 2 for AP2, and A = 3 for AP3.The prefix 1 here denotes that the VLAN carries IP traffic. For example the three VLANs on any SN will be 11 for AP1, 12 for AP2 and 13 for AP3.
- The NAPs and AUXs had VLAN ids 21, 22 and 23.The prefix 2 here denotes that the VLAN carries ICN traffic.
- The VLAN10 was reserved for management and had a scope that was limited to within an SN.

Thus, since a directive antenna's wired NIC was directly connected to the router, it had a VLAN10 and VLAN2XY (Prefix 2 denoting that the VLAN carries ICN traffic and X is the lower SN number; Y the higher SN number). On the other hand, since the directive antenna's wireless NIC was pointed towards a similar NIC on another super node, it had interfaces corresponding to 1XY (Prefix 1 denoting that the VLAN carries IP traffic and X is the lower SN number; Y the higher SN number)) and 2XY (Prefix 2 denoting that the VLAN carries ICN traffic and X is the lower SN number; Y the higher SN number). In the access point's sectorial antennas, only the wired NIC had interfaces corresponding to the VLANs 10 and 1A (A=1 for AP1, A=2 for AP2, and A=3 for AP3) for similar reasons as the directive antenna. Finally, in the router, interfaces corresponding to VLAN10 were defined on all the ports

We organized the bridges within a router on an SN as follows (Fig. 4 and Fig. 5):

Routers

- A bridge br1YZ for each VLAN1YZ. Each bridge only has one port and VLAN1YZ connected to the corresponding directive antenna. For example, in Fig. 5 br112 has port P1 and VLAN112 connected to a directive antenna.
- A bridge br2YZ for each VLAN2YZ. Each bridge has two ports and VLAN2YZ connected to the corresponding directive antenna and the switch of the ICN fabric network. For example, in Fig. 5 br212 has two ports P1 and P5 and VLAN212. Port P1's VLAN212 is connected to the directive antenna. Port P5's VLAN212 is connected to a switch in the ICN fabric network.
- A bridge br1A for each VLAN1A. Each bridge may only have one port and VLAN1A connected to the corresponding AP. For example, in Fig. 5, br11 has port P6 and VLAN11 connected to the AP provided by the sectorial antenna.
- A bridge br2A for each VLAN2A. Each bridge has at least one port and VLAN2A connected to the switch in the ICN fabric network. For example, in Fig. 5, br21 has port P5 and VLAN21 connected to the switch in the ICN fabric network.
- A bridge br10 for VLAN10 connected to all ports and VLAN10. For example, in Fig. 5, br10 is connected to all ports namely P1, P5, and P6 as well as to VLAN10.

FWDs

- An OpenVSwitch (OVS) based software switch runs on each forwarder. Each such switch has exactly one bridge called br1.

CLEs

– A bridge called br-cli for the LXC. It has the corresponding VLAN1A and all the LXCs' interfaces.

We had two separate deployments as discussed earlier. In the lab deployment, we had three SNs whereas in the production network in the villages, we had six SNs. We organized the IP assignments as follows:

– A 10.X/16 IPv4 block per deployment.
– A 10.X.Y/24 IPv4 block per SN.
– The 10.X.Y.0/26 IPv4 block per SN for management IPs. All devices except end-user equipment have management IP.
– The 10.X.Y.64/26 IPv4 block per SN for AP1 clients. The 10.X.Y.128/26 IPv4 block per SN for AP2 clients. The 10.X.Y.192/26 IPv4 block per SN for AP3 clients.
– In the CDs, the management IPs have a dedicated routing table.

In our design the backbone is IP-ICN dual stack but each AP can only be associated to one of the two network underlays at a time (either IP or ICN). The association to one of the networks is implemented at the router level by associating the corresponding VLAN1A to either the br1A bridge or to the br2A bridge.

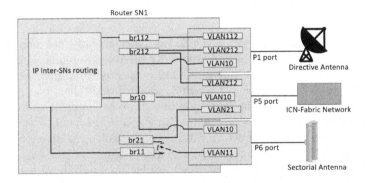

Fig. 5. Arrangement to switch between ICN and IP on SN1.

Consider Fig. 5 where we show the organization of VLAN tags, bridges and physical ports in the router on Super Node 1. The user traffic is sent and received on the physical port P6 via the sectorial antenna and is passed on to the sub-interface corresponding to VLAN11. This is the traffic that can then be switched either to the bridge br11 resulting in the user network connecting to the IP network or to bridge br21 resulting in the user network being connected to the ICN network. In this way, we were able to provide customers with highly available Internet services even when the ICN network was being debugged for crashes or performance issues by associating UE to the ICN or the IP network at the AP level.

Solution to Problem 3. We now discuss the causes of the emergent behavior described in the previous section and outline the general techniques and processes that practitioners can adopt to run ICN and IP-based networks over the same infrastructure.

One of the causes of the emergent behavior described in the previous section is that many of the default settings in the operator's network infrastructure are not the correct settings for the ICN software to operate upon. These settings then interact unpredictably with the deployed ICN network. Moreover, it was tedious and time consuming to debug the emergent behaviors during deployment because of an incomplete capturing and enforcement of the precedence relations between the configuration of the network operator and those of the ICN deployer. We now explain the strategies that we adopted to deal with these issues.

Issue 1. Emergent behavior caused by the default settings of software that were only appropriate for an IP and not an ICN network:
As described earlier, on each Supernode, we set up an OVS switch in software running on a Linux box with a single bridge having multiple ports. Each of the multiple ports correspond to a different VLAN. This bridge by default, constructs in its table a so-called 'normal rule'. Such a rule has an action that forwards all traffic from one port on the bridge to all the other ports on the bridge. This is the default configuration of an OVS switch for an IP network.

However, this created loops involving broadcast/multicast MAC frames circulating in the various VLANs leading to a complete network meltdown with even SSH access becoming impossible. Thus, we were unable to even run our script to deploy the ICN network.

Solution to Issue 1. To solve this issue, a single line of code was needed to keep the table of OVS initially empty.

The result of the line of code is a new default behavior of the bridge where it does not forward any packet arriving at a port to any other port. This caused the looping issue to disappear and we could run the ICN deployment tool. This tool wrote new rules onto the OVS-switch's bridge and we were able to deploy our ICN network.

As multiple virtual switches become common in Network Function Virtualization and network slicing based scenarios with complex topologies, looping issues will become all pervasive. Thus, setting up a virtual switch with appropriate initialization strategies until rules are written to it by an SDN controller has become important in a real deployment.

In another default Linux settings, the kernel offloads TCP segmentation to the NIC for better IP network performance.

However, this resulted in our NAP Blackadder application getting larger packets than it expected because the NIC was not respecting the MTU size set in the NAP code. The NAP would drop these larger than expected packets resulting in a packet loss and a subsequent re- transmission of the packet from the sender. The overall effect was that the throughput between a sender and a receiver was observed to be between 0.5 Mbps and 1.5 Mbps on our ICN network.

A simple solution that we adapted was to switch off the TCP segmentation offload configuration of the Linux kernel on which the NAP was running. This caused the throughput between the same sender and receiver to jump to around 18 Mbps from the initial 0.5 Mbps to 1.5 Mbps.

For increased network performance in operational deployments, the operators utilize many optimizations. Therefore, any real-life deployment that seeks to retain the HTTP/IP configuration of end-user devices while at the same time replacing the standard TCP/Internet Protocols (IPs) network stack in the internal network must carefully consider the impact of such optimizations on the operational parameters.

Issue 2: Difficulties in debugging emergent behavior during deployment caused by an incomplete capture and enforcement of the precedence relations between the configuration of the network operator and that of the ICN deployer:
The root of this problem lies in the fact that even when the ICN and IP networks are isolated, these two network stacks must be setup on the same machines resulting in the afore-mentioned constraints and making it tedious and error prone to track down the bugs causing the emergent behavior.

Solution to Issue 2. We now discuss our initial workflow and how we modified it to make it easier for us to deal with the emergent behavior and point out the sources of precedence constraints that we had to deal with for a successful deployment.

Initially, the entire network infrastructure including setting up of all the hardware and the software (excluding ICN software) was deemed to be the concern of the network operator. Once the infrastructure was setup, the ICN deployer would deploy the software stack for ICN on the network infrastructure.

However, this caused difficulties in debugging emergent behavior. It was often unclear if an emergent behavior (say network meltdown) was caused by a configuration error in the network operator's deployment or in the configuration of the ICN software or in an interaction between the two.

So, instead of following a workflow where the network operator completes their configuration and then hands over the deployment of ICN software to the ICN deployer, we changed it. In the new workflow, we decided to interleave the steps that the network operator and the ICN deployer were implementing for the deployment in a single script. This enabled us to explicitly represent the precedence relations between the network operator's and the ICN deployer's configurations in that script. A side effect was that both the network operator and the ICN deployer became aware of the other's precedence constraints making it easier to debug emergent behavior.

These precedence constraints arise out of the dependency of the ICN network elements on the configuration and initialization of machines on which they are hosted. These dependencies can be a result of the requirement of an ICN component for data so that it can set up its execution environment within the operating system running on a machine and the network to which that machine is connected. Some examples include:

a) Topology Manager (TM) needs to know what paths are available for the ICN traffic. These link layer paths are then used by the TM to calculate the topology of the network. The TM can only be set through the IP management network. Thus, the VLANs and IP network interfaces must be set up before the TM can function properly.
b) Rendezvous (RV) and TM can only run if the ICN component called Blackadder (the ICN pub/sub forwarder) is already running. Blackadder in turn can only run if the operating system has been installed, configured and running in the operator's machine. This installation of Blackadder is done via the IP management network. These constraints are imposed by the architecture specifying that RV and TM are at a higher layer compared to Blackadder (See Sect. 2).
c) RV can match subscriptions to publications only if the operator network is up and running.

Another source of a precedence constraint is the requirement that a component must wait for another component to finish its initialization before starting its own configuration. This initialization often takes time that cannot be precisely predicted. Some examples from our deployment include:

a) The scripts initializing the ICN Blackadder component need to wait for an imprecise duration of time whilst the operating system and the network is booted up.
b) The RV, TM initialization by the scripts must wait for the ICN Blackadder bootup to finish. Knowing that RV, TM need to boot up after ICN Blackadder is not enough. Additionally, the scripts initializing RV, TM must wait for an imprecise duration of time as ICN Blackadder is booted up.

We now discuss ways to enforce the precedence constraints to avoid unpredictable emergent behavior during the initialization of the ICN network. Note that once the ICN network is initialized, the responsibility to ensure that runtime precedence constraints within the ICN network are respected lies with the various ICN protocols and the design of its architecture.

When the initialization of a component depends on data from the operating system or a network element that themselves need to be initialized, we need to capture these dependencies in a precedence graph. This precedence graph can be an informal diagram or expressed in code. The precedence graph can then be used to extract a schedule informally, or by running an algorithm such as topological sort on the precedence graph. For complex deployments, more sophisticated algorithms such as the critical path method can be considered to generate the schedule.

We generated such a schedule informally by carefully walking through the order in which the ICN and IP components needed to be initialized. For example, our schedule encapsulated in scripts made sure that the network interfaces were set up in all machines for both the ICN and IP networks before we deployed the configuration and topology of the ICN network. The schedule took care of the precedence constraint requirement of an ICN component for getting data so that it can set up its execution environment within the operating system running on a machine and the network to which that machine is connected.

We also made sure that the scripts encoding this schedule would wait for a configuration to finish before initiating the next configuration. This was done via remote configuration calls to the appropriate machines that would sleep long enough so that the configuration on the remote machine was completed. This took care of the precedence constraint requirement that a component must wait an unpredictable duration of time for another component to finish its initialization before starting its own configuration.

Thus, we were able to reduce the problem of dealing with the unpredictable emergent behavior during initialization due to the interaction between ICN software and the IP software to one of dealing with generating initialization schedule from precedence constraints using standard techniques and algorithms.

Solution to Problem 4, 5, 6. To solve the requirement for an appropriate workflow between the ICN deployer and the network operator as discussed in Sect. 3 above, we centered the workflow around code that encapsulated the deployment.

This code became the interface for interaction between the ICN deployer and the network operator. All the necessary configurations of various software components, network interfaces, SDN switches being used for both ICN and IP were initialized by this code. Thus, the code became both the documentation of the configuration as well as of the schedule of re-deployment in case of crashes, performance issues etc. As a result, both the ICN deployer and the network operator could go through the code together and agree on the necessary changes needed to address a problem. Note that once the infrastructure is captured by code, it is easy to modularize the code with a module corresponding to one component of deployment say the NAP. Capturing the various component versions in the code made the re- deployment repeatable and deterministic.

Moreover, using the code in this way to represent the IP and ICN infrastructure made it possible to use standard software development processes to coordinate between the ICN deployer and the network operator. For example, in order to update a software component, we would change the version of the deployment code thereby easily maintaining a record of working deployments in the previous versions.

Additionally, we followed good software engineering practices for naming variables in code. The VLANs, network interfaces, antenna etc. were named in a systematic and consistent manner as already discussed. These names were then easily used in discussions between the ICN deployer and the network operator without any ambiguity as part of the workflow.

Using the code as a representation of infrastructure also enabled us to automate the process of recovery in case of software/hardware crashes. The code that was being used to monitor various components would generate the necessary log files and would automatically run the deployment scripts whenever a component crashed.

Another advantage of making code as the interface between the ICN deployer and the network operator was that we could make changes in small increments (For example adding or removing computing devices) and could easily undo things if software components crashed or performed poorly. Similarly, the network operator could easily switch from ICN to IP secure in the knowledge that ICN configuration was being reworked in the code and would be easily re-deployed. This also enabled us to provide a high degree of availability of the internet service to the customers.

We also partially replicated the field trial by setting up three Super Nodes in our lab in Barcelona. All the software components, computing devices, routers, switches used in this lab setup were identical to the ones that we used in the trial. The code that encapsulated the deployment was always first tested in the lab whenever we wanted to change the configuration of the deployment software/hardware. This ensured that any bugs were caught, and our customers were assured of a high availability of Internet services.

The code described above was run from a centralized server that was accessible to both the ICN deployer and the network operator. This ensured that both the deployer and operator could redeploy the entire system on their own since all the configuration knowledge was already captured in the code.

Thus, by representing the deployment infrastructure as code, accessible to both the deployer and the operator and properly versioned, we were able to use the code as the interface between the deployer and operator. The practices we have described above are a subset of the practices called *Infrastructure as Code* being advocated by the DevOPs community for cloud deployments [26]. Each of the practice that we have described above is on its own already known and well established. However, when these practices are combined, we get emergent behavior that is useful in deployments such as ours. In particular, it enabled us to ensure a smooth workflow that minimized downtime for the customers.

5   Requirements

We now summarize the lessons learned and propose the following requirements as constraining guidelines that could be used by other researchers looking to deploy their ICN/alternative network architecture in a real-world operational network based on the dual-stack approach and to develop tools for such deployments. These requirements represent constraints that when followed lead to tractable deployments of reduced complexity. This complexity of deployment is caused by the problems that we discussed in Sect. 3 of this paper. Besides, these requirements are general enough to be useful for deployment of network layers other than ICN using a similar dual-stack approach.

Requirement 1. *Translate novelties of ICN/alternative architecture into familiar configurations for the network operator.* A deployment network involves many network technicians who might be unfamiliar with experimental architectures and may be skeptical about using them.

One way to deal with this problem is running training workshops for them to make them familiar with such an architecture.

However, often the time allocated to run the ICN/alternative software is limited due to commercial/usability considerations- in our case we were given a 3-month window to set up the network and deploy the ICN software. Moreover, the network technicians are often required to be available on demand for the day-to-day running of their operational network. This often makes it infeasible in terms of time to run training workshops for them to be familiarized with a new technique.

Therefore, we suggest that the instructions given to the technicians for deployment must translate the novelties of an architecture into configuration techniques that they already know whenever possible. The tools developed should have an interface that supports those configuration techniques. In our case this entailed providing the network operator's technicians with semantically meaningful scheme of VLAN tags and allowing them to easily switch between VLANs. This switching of VLANs by the technicians translated into switching between IP and ICN at the deployer's level.

Requirement 2. *Use precedence relations as a centerpiece of a strategy to deal with emergent behavior.* In a deployment network, prolonged network down-times are unacceptable to the customers. However, since ICN/alternative networks are not as highly engineered as the IP network, unpredictable emergent behavior that degrades the customer experience is inevitable.

Debugging such emergent behavior is tedious and time consuming. The technicians on the field are not familiar with the ICN/alternative network technology making it hard for them to debug emergent behavior. As a result, minimizing the time required to debug emergent behavior as and when it is encountered is critical in an operational network as opposed to a research network.

Therefore, debugging emergent properties in a systematic way using precedence relations should become the centerpiece of the deployment workflow. The precedence relations between components should be treated as a first-class entity for deployment tools to deal with the unpredictable emergent behavior. This means that the deployment tools should be centered around generating an appropriate initialization schedule from those precedence relations using techniques such as topological sort, critical path etc.

Requirement 3. *Represent Infrastructure as Code.* The entire deployment and its schedule as generated above should be captured in code that is supported by tools. This code then becomes the interface between the ICN/alternative network deployer and the network operator.

In particular, attention should be paid to the naming of various hardware/software components to avoid ambiguity when dealing with system failures. The component's versions and their updates must only be done via this code (rather than logging into individual machines) in order to document them and to be able to easily detect changes that broke the deployment. This code itself should be properly versioned to capture all the working deployments and simplify a roll-back to previous configurations. This code should be tested on a replica of the actual deployment to detect any problems early. The code itself should be run from a machine that is accessible to both the deployer and the operator.

All these practices taken together result in the emergence of a smooth workflow between the ICN deployer and the network operator.

Requirement 4. *Retain IP as the fallback network.* Live deployments of IP networks are highly engineered to optimize for an acceptable user experience. However, ICN/alternative networks will inevitably be not as robust and might fail from time to time.

Therefore it is highly recommended that tools should provide an easy way to switch traffic between IP and ICN/alternative network to deal with unforeseen problems in the ICN/alternative network.

6   Related Work

To the best of our knowledge, outside our work, there have been no field deployments of ICN involving real users that provided an easy switch between IP and ICN when required. There are four styles of experimental ICN deployment configurations [22] that have been discussed in the literature. These include wholesale replacement of IP by ICN [1–3], ICN deployed as an overlay [3–6], ICN deployed as an underlay -both in the core network [7–9, 19–21] and in the edge network [10–12] and finally, ICN-as-a-slice [13]. We deployed ICN in the field with real users as an underlay in the core network as part of the RIFE [9] and POINT [7] project mentioned above, and this paper discusses the practical lessons learnt from the exercise.

In addition we wanted that the ICN should also run in parallel with an IP-based management network over the same physical infrastructure (See Fig. 2). This management network was required so that we could install/update software components, debug, run diagnostic software such as IPerf etc. We used L2 network virtualization (VLAN) to enable such a parallel operation.

There are many examples of using network virtualization to multiplex between various networks and run them in parallel over a shared physical infrastructure. Tempest [14] proposed running many virtual Asynchronous Transfer Mode (ATM)s over the same physical infrastructure. The authors in [15] advocated using a network of overlay tunnels to support multiple networks. Overlay architectures such as PlanetLab [16] and GENI [17] have been used to run different kinds of networks over a common physical substrate. Techniques of slicing a physical network into multiple virtual networks using SDN technology have also been proposed [18]. However, none of these projects ran ICN and IP in parallel using VLAN in a network being used by real users as we have done.

The *Infrastructure as Code* movement has emerged as a way to deal with the complexities of cloud deployment within the DevOps community [26]. Although many of the practices we used are a subset of the practices being advocated there, our deployments dealt with the specific problem of running ICN and IP stacks together rather than the deployment of cloud-based infrastructure such as VMs, containers etc. which has been the focus of the *Infrastructure as Code* movement.

7   Conclusions

The main concern of this paper has been to discuss general strategies to deal with emergent behavior. These strategies reduce ICN/alternative network deployment times in an operational network that is traditionally optimized for the semantics of IP. The strategies we suggest involve following a dual stack approach and encapsulating the deployed infrastructure in code. We advocate paying particular attention to integrating the code with the workflow between the ICN deployer and the network operator. The order in which the various software/hardware components of the infrastructure are deployed should be generated out of the precedence constraints of those components. The design of this workflow should include an operationally easy way to switch between the ICN and IP network while being minimally disruptive to the customers.

We hope that the general requirements presented in this paper will prove useful as constraining guidelines to develop tools for ICN and other alternative network layer deployments and compliment the ongoing discussions within the Information-Centric Networking Research Group (ICNRG) of the Internet Research Task Force (IRTF). Additionally, we hope that this paper contributes to a set of best practices for the development of tools that are useful at the lowest level of abstraction for designing an Internetwork [23].

Acknowledgement. We want to thank Dr. Dirk Trossen, Huawei, Munich, Ulises Olvera-Hernandz, Interdigital Europe and Dr. Leandro Navarro UPC Barcelona for the many useful suggestions and comments they gave during the preparation of this manuscript.

References

1. NFD Homepage. https://named-data.net/doc/NFD/current/. Accessed 13 Oct 2020
2. Jacobson, V., et al.: Networking named content. In: Proceedings of the 5th International Conference on Emerging Networking Experiments and Technologies CoNEXT 2009, pp. 1–12. https://doi.org/10.1145/1658939.1658941
3. Trossen, D., Parisis, G.: Designing and realizing an information-centric internet. IEEE Commun. Mag. **50**(7), 60–67 (2012). https://doi.org/10.1109/MCOM.2012.6231280
4. PARC, CCNx Over UDP. https://www.ietf.org/proceedings/interim-2015-icnrg-04/slides/slides-interim-2015-icnrg-4-5.pdf. Accessed 13 Oct 2020

5. Hybrid ICN Cisco: Cisco Announces Important Steps toward Adoption of Information-Centric Networking. https://blogs.cisco.com/sp/cisco-announces-important-steps-toward-adoption-of-information-centric-networking. Accessed 13 Oct 2020
6. Kutscher, D., Farrell, S., Davies E.: The NetInf Protocol. Internet-Draft draft-kutscher-icnrg-netinf-proto-01 (2013). https://tools.ietf.org/html/draft-kutscher-icnrg-netinf-proto-01. Accessed 13 Oct 2020
7. Trossen, D., Reed, M., Riihijarvi, J., Georgiades, M., Fotiou, N., Xylomenos, P.: POINT: IP over ICN - the better IP? In: European Conference on Networks and Communications (EuCNC) (2015). https://doi.org/10.1109/EuCNC.2015.7194109
8. White, G., Rutz, G.: Content delivery with content centric networking, White Paper. CableLabs (2010). https://www.cablelabs.com/wp-content/uploads/2016/02/Content-Delivery-with-Content-Centric-Networking-Feb-2016.pdf. Accessed 13 Oct 2020
9. RIFE Homepage. https://www.rife-project.eu/. Accessed 2 June 2020
10. Zhang, Y., et al.: Design Considerations for Applying ICN to IoT. Internet-Draft draft-zhang-icnrg-icniot-01 (2017). https://tools.ietf.org/id/draft-irtf-icnrg-icniot-01.html. Accessed 13 Oct 2020
11. Ravindran, R., Liu, X., Chakraborti, A., Zhang, X., Wang, G.: Towards software defined ICN based edge-cloud services. In: IEEE International Conference on CloudNetworking (CloudNet) (2013). https://doi.org/10.1109/CloudNet.2013.6710583
12. Azgin, A., Ravindran, R., Chakraborti, A., Wang, G.: Seamless mobility as a service. In: Information-Centric Networks, ACM ICN Sigcomm, IC5G Workshop (2016). https://doi.org/10.1145/2984356.2988521
13. Ravindran, R., Chakraborti, A., Amin, S., Azgin, A., Wang, G.: 5G-ICN: delivering ICN services over 5G using network slicing. IEEE Commun. Mag. **55** (2016). https://doi.org/10.1109/MCOM.2017.1600938
14. Van Der Merwe, J.E., Rooney, S., Leslie, L., Crosby, S.: The tempest-a practical framework for network programmability. IEEE Netw. **12**(3), 20–28 (1998). https://doi.org/10.1109/65.690958
15. Bavier, A., Feamster, N., Huang, M., Peterson, L., Rexford, J.: In VINI veritas: realistic and controlled network experimentation. ACM SIGCOMM Comput. Commun. Rev. **36**(4), 3–14 (2006). https://doi.org/10.1145/1151659.1159916
16. Peterson, L., Anderson, T., Culler, D., Roscoe, T.: A blueprint for introducing disruptive technology into the Internet. ACM SIGCOMM Comput. Commun. Rev. **33**(1), 59–64 (2003). https://doi.org/10.1145/774763.774772
17. Peterson, L., et al.: GENI design principles. IEEE Comput. **39**(9), 102–105 (2006)
18. Yiakoumis, Y., Kok-Kiong, Y., Katti, S., Parulkar, G., McKeown, N.: Slicing home networks. In: Proceedings of the 2nd ACM SIGCOMM Workshop on Home Networks. ACM (2011). https://doi.org/10.1145/2018567.2018569
19. Susmit, S. Fan, C., White, G.: Bridging the ICN Deployment Gap with IPoC: an IP-over-ICN protocol for 5G Networks. In: Proceedings of the 2018 Workshop on Networking for Emerging Applications and Technologies. ACM (2018). https://doi.org/10.1145/3229574.3229575
20. Refaei, T., Ma, J., Ha, S., Liu, S.: Integrating IP and NDN through an extensible IP-NDN gateway. In: Proceedings of the 4th ACM Conference on Information-Centric Networking. ACM, New York, pp. 224–225 (2017). https://doi.org/10.1145/3125719.3132112

21. Moiseenko, I., Dave Oran, D.: TCP/ICN: carrying TCP over content centric and named data networks. In: Proceedings of the 3rd ACM Conference on Information-Centric Networking. ACM, New York, pp. 112–121 (2016). https://doi.org/10.1145/2984356.2984357
22. Rahman, A., Trossen, D., Kutscher, D., Ravindran, R.: Deployment considerations for information-centric networking (ICN) ICNRG draft (2019). https://tools.ietf.org/html/rfc8763. Accessed 13 Oct 2020
23. Clark, D.D.: Designing an Internet. MIT Press (2018)
24. Baig, R., Freitag, F., Navarro, L.: Cloudy in guifi.net: establishing and sustaining a community cloud as open commons. Future Gener. Comput. Syst. (2018). https://doi.org/10.1016/j.future.2017.12.017
25. Baig, R., Roca, R., Freitag, F., Navarro, L.: guifi.net, a crowdsourced network infrastructure held in common. Comput. Netw. 90, 150–165 (2015). https://doi.org/10.1016/j.comnet.2015.07.009
26. Kief, M.: Infrastructure as Code: Managing Servers in the Cloud. O'Reilly Media, Inc. (2016)

A Pure Network-Based Approach to Achieve Always Best Quality Video Streaming

Toan Nguyen-Duc[✉], Xuan Doan-Thanh, and Hung Do-Viet

Hanoi University of Science and Technology, Hanoi, Vietnam
xuan.doanthanh@hust.edu.vn

Abstract. The demand for video streaming has been more and more increasing, causing the streaming technology and the related technologies to be improved to meet the requirement of the best quality of experience (QoE) from various users. A lot of research has been focusing on studying users' behavior or developing streaming client and/or server application. These works estimate the network state passively and are lack of a global view of the network. As a result, they meet difficulty in bandwidth competition, QoE fairness scenarios. Some works optimize routing mechanism to improve video quality and QoE. This work also proposes a pure network-based approach, however taking into account the characteristics of video streaming application, to support an always best QoE to end-users. The proposed approach leverages the advantage of SDN network to convert the explored characteristic of streaming application into the network configuration. The proposal has been implemented on a real testbed. The obtained results show that the proposed mechanism has maintained the best video quality while maximizing the bandwidth for competitor application, i.e., file download using ftp protocol.

Keywords: HTTP adaptive streaming · QoE fairness · Bandwidth competition · Software-defined networks

1 Introduction

Video streaming is one of the most popular services on the Internet. The demand for high-quality videos is growing exponentially. Cisco [1] estimates that the amount of video traffic will be about 37 exabytes (EB) per month. Therefore, video streaming techniques have been examined and improved. Along with the demands for high-quality videos is the demand for the best Quality of Experience (QoE). This is still an open challenge for the Internet network manager since the Internet was originally designed for the best-effort, non-real-time data transmission.

To this end, many research efforts focus on studying users' behavior, improving system architecture, proposing handover mechanisms, developing video streaming client and server application, optimizing network routing algorithms. It is clear that to understand the user experience directly is the most straight and effective way to improve QoE. However, this method may violate the users' privacy. Several researches [1–3] have

© ICST Institute for Computer Sciences, Social Informatics and Telecommunications Engineering 2021
Published by Springer Nature Switzerland AG 2021. All Rights Reserved
Y. Weng et al. (Eds.): TridentCom 2020, LNICST 380, pp. 47–58, 2021.
https://doi.org/10.1007/978-3-030-77428-8_4

studied the behavior of adaptive streaming application to provide an adaptive bitrate mechanism. The authors in [3] rely on a special mobility server acts as a video cache server at the edge network to adjust the video bitrate. The cached video may not contain all quality versions, leading video clients to download popular downloaded video segments, not their desired ones. The authors in [1, 2] estimate the network state based on the buffer on the client side. These works estimate the network state passively and lack of a global view of the network. As a result, they meet difficulty in bandwidth competition, QoE fairness scenarios.

It is possible to control quality of video streaming application only from network domain. The authors in [4] proposed a software-define infrastructure to assist the adaptive bitrate in video streaming. Their proposal monitors the state of network device to select the best cache in the network. Then, they modify the adaptive bitrate algorithm on the video client. This work did not consider the scenario where the video streaming application has to compete bandwidth with other application. For this purpose, many researches [5–7] have tried to maximize the QoE of multiple clients in a shared network environment. The authors in [5] focused on QoE fairness among multiple video clients. The video clients run on devices with various resolutions, hence the received experience for users are quite different. The work in [6] considered the scenario where a large number of video client share the same network. An external application was developed to communicate with the controller about the requirement per video client. The work in [7] is the most relevant to our proposal. The authors [7] consider the bandwidth competition between HAS and other application. They focus on estimating the QoE based on the collected QoS values. The estimated QoE is then used to control the network. However, this work did not consider the characteristic of the HAS application in controlling the network.

Different from existing studies, this work explores the details of HAS application behavior to provide a suitable network control, aiming to maintain the best QoE for video player while maximizing the available bandwidth for other application. The proposed mechanism has been implemented on a real testbed. The experiments represent a reality situation where video traffic has to compete for bandwidth with greedy TCP flows, i.e., file download. The obtained results show that the proposed mechanism satisfy both type of users. The video was always delivered with the best quality. Also, the time for downloading file was 15.5 s. This duration is shorter more than ten percent in comparison with the case our mechanism was not used.

The rest of the paper is organized as follows: In Sect. 2, the background of this work including basics of HTTP Adaptive streaming, the behavior of HAS application and SDN technologies will be described. In Sect. 3, the proposed algorithm will be explained. Section 4 will describe the evaluation on the performance of the system. Finally, the paper will be concluded in Sect. 5.

2 Background

2.1 HTTP Adaptive Streaming (HAS)

In HAS, video contents are split into small segments of a certain length. Each segment is encoded in several predefined qualities. A combination of resolution, frame rate, bitrate, etc., determines such quality. MPEG-DASH describes these characteristics of the segments in a file called Media Presentation Description (MPD), which is an Extensible Markup Language (XML) file. The segments and the MPD file are then hosted on the server. Before a streaming session is started, the client requests the MPD file through an HTTP GET request. Based on the information in this file, segment requests can be sent to the media server. To request a suitable segment size, the client has to measure the available bandwidth to estimate the condition of the end-to-end connectivity. Based on the estimated available bandwidth and playout buffer conditions, the client determines the suitable bitrate and requests the appropriate video segments by sending HTTP GET requests. Once a segment is entirely downloaded, the next segment is requested. The received segments are individually decoded and are played in sequence.

2.2 Exploring HAS Application's Behavior

When an end-user is watching HAS-based videos, video segments are regularly downloaded. To download a segment, the client sends a GET request to the server. If the client detects that the network throughput is getting worse enough, i.e., below a threshold, then the resolution and bitrate of the video segment in the GET request will reduce.

In scenario A, a measurement of video streaming in a stable state is conducted. Here, the stable state is defined that there is no competition from other users, only one network user, and the network capacity is fast enough to stream videos at the highest speed. The considered metric is the average duration between 2 consecutive GET requests. The obtained average duration between 2 consecutive GET requests is 4.003 s.

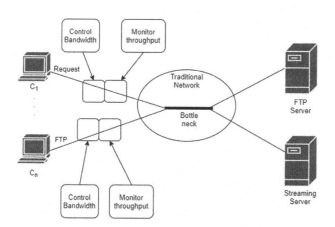

Fig. 1. HAS competes bandwidth in a traditional network

In scenario B, video streaming and other TCP-based application, i.e., File download using FTP protocol, generally share a bottleneck link; hence, they have to compete for bandwidth as shown in Fig. 1. The measured results are given in Fig. 2, the video quality was reduced from 1920 × 1080 pixels to 1280 × 720 pixels. Also, the average duration between 2 consecutive GET requests changed to 7.17 s. The average duration to download a 10-MB file was 17.29 s. This download duration is 9 s longer than that obtained when the file was downloaded in the stable state.

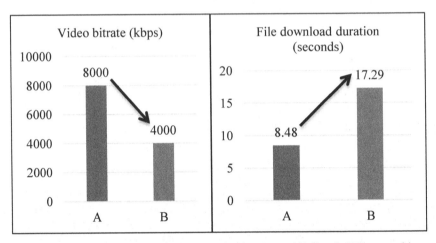

Fig. 2. HAS behavior in two scenarios: A. Stable state and B. Bandwidth competition

2.3 Software-Defined Network (SDN)

In an SDN-based network, the SDN controller knows the network wide information including the network topology as given in Fig. 3. Hence, it potentially allocates a suitable bandwidth for each connection. The problem is that the SDN controller only works with SDN switch, it does not communicate with the hosts. Therefore, the SDN controller is unable to understand the hosts' requirement. This work will propose a mechanism to address this issue.

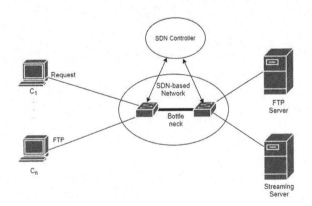

Fig. 3. HAS in an SDN-based network

3 Our Proposed Mechanism

As mentioned in Sect. 2.1, during a streaming process, the video client periodically sends GET requests to the server. Each GET request is sent in a packet. In each packet, parameters including video bitrate and video resolution are requested. The value of the required parameters is based on the estimation of the connectivity state, i.e., the estimated available bandwidth.

Once the GET request is sent, if the requested video segment is available, it will be downloaded to the client. In general, all video segments have the same duration, however, each segment has a different frame rate causing the size of each segment to be different. Therefore, the duration to download a segment will vary depending on the size of the segment. Short segments are good to adapt quickly to bandwidth changes and prevent stalls, but longer segments may have a better encoding efficiency and quality. The segment length recommended for DASH is around 2 to 4 s [8]. Therefore, a duration of 4 s has been chosen as the segment length, which is a good compromise between encoding efficiency and flexibility for stream adaption to bandwidth changes.

The HAS application behavior will be modeled in the following section.

3.1 Modeling HAS Application Behavior

To capture application traffic, every packet has been sniffed. All the packets belonging to the monitored application are filtered. The collected information is stored in text files. The monitoring procedure for the GET requests is as follows (Fig. 4):

```
GET interface from keyboard
IF interface:
   sniff(filter="port 80", prn=process_packet, iface=iface)
ELSE using default interface:
   sniff(filter="port 80", prn=process_packet, store=False)
ENDIF

FUNCTION process packet(packet):
IF packet is an HTTP Request:
   Get the requested URL
   Get the source and destination IP Address of the requester

   Get the request method
   method <- packet[HTTPRequest].Method.decode
   dateTimeObj <- now
   Turn up a timer
   IF method is "GET":
      Write the packet's information to a file
   ENDIF
ENDFUNCTION
```

Fig. 4. Pseudo code of the monitoring procedure

After the duration between 2 consecutive GET requests has been studied. The video streaming behavior within a duration is modeled as illustrated in Fig. 5.

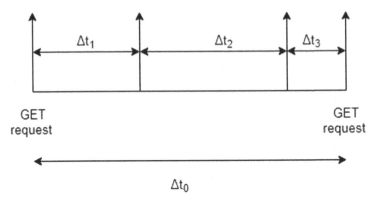

Fig. 5. Video streaming behavior

The Fig. 5 shows that Δt_0 is the duration between 2 consecutive GET requests. Within Δt_0, Δt_1 is the duration for the client to download the segment, Δt_3 is the duration for the client to detect connectivity condition, and Δt_2 is the duration that the video client may not consume the network bandwidth.

3.2 Considered Bandwidth Competition Scenario

In this work, a client requests the video resolution from a video streaming server. It is assumed that the bandwidth competition occurs after the client sends request for the highest video quality as shown in Fig. 6.

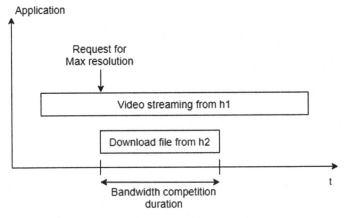

Fig. 6. Considered scenario

The duration of file downloading is assumed to be not as long as the same mechanism could be applied repeatedly for long duration cases. Due to the native TCP congestion control, all applications will have to share the available bandwidth fairly. As a result, the video client may have to request a lower video resolution if the bandwidth is lower than a threshold. Also, the duration to download file is longer.

3.3 Proposed Mechanism in Bandwidth Competition Scenario

The proposed algorithm to control network in case of bandwidth competition is given in Fig. 7. While video is streaming from the video server to the video client, a module written in python is to monitor video segment requests from the video client. When the maximum video resolution has been requested, the module to handle bandwidth competition is invoked. The module bandwidth competition handle takes the model of application behavior as the input to translate into network configuration to control the network in 3 consecutive GET requests.

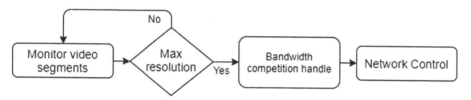

Fig. 7. Algorithm to control network in bandwidth competition scenario

The mechanism of the bandwidth competition handle is as follows: After the video client sends the GET request for the maximum resolution, it is necessary to provide enough bandwidth for the video client to download the segment. In this duration, the bandwidth for the other application will be limited. Once the video segment is downloaded, the bandwidth for the video application can be reduced. This duration is an opportunity for other applications to have maximized available bandwidth. The bandwidth allocation for the video application must be increased before the client starts detecting network conditions. This means bandwidth for other applications must be reduced.

4 Evaluation

4.1 Experiment Setup

The topology of the experiments is shown in Fig. 8.

In this topology, three hosts emulated by Mininet connect to a real server via an emulated switch s1. The switch can be controlled by an SDN controller, however, in this work, the network operates without any controllers. The interface eth0 of the host h1, the interface eth0 of the host h2, and the interface eth0 of the host h3 are connected to port 1, port 2, port 3 of the switch s1, respectively. The bandwidth between h1 and s1 is $B1-1$, the bandwidth between h2 and s1 is $B1-2$, and the bandwidth between h3 and s1 is $B1-3$. The bandwidth between s1 and the server is Bs-s. Each of this bandwidth can be set individually to any values. Initially, all of them are set to 10 Mbps.

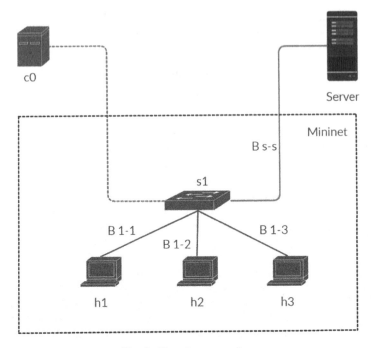

Fig. 8. Experiment topology

Figure 8 also shows that hosts emulated by Mininet connect to a real server via an emulated switch. Mininet hosts can communicate with a real server by using NAT technology. The operating system of the server is Windows version 10 64bit. On the server, the built-in Internet Information Services (IIS) is used as a Web Server to stream video via HTTP protocol. The videos used in the experiment is from [9] have characteristics as given in Table 1.

To stream video, two tools, namely MP4Box and MP4Client, of an open-source framework called GPAC [10], have been used. MP4Box was used for the preparation of HTTP Adaptive Streaming content; while MP4Client is used as a video player. The model to stream video adaptively from a server to a client is described in Fig. 9. The video contents generated by the video streaming server are put into a web server. These contents are streamed to the video player at the client via HTTP protocol.

Table 1. Video file characteristics

Filename	Frame rate	Resolution	Bit rate
bbb_30fps_320 × 180_200k.mp4	30 fps	320 × 180 pixels	200 kbps
bbb_30fps_320 × 180_400k.mp4	30 fps	320 × 180 pixels	400 kbps
bbb_30fps_480 × 270_600k.mp4	30 fps	480 × 270 pixels	600 kbps
bbb_30fps_640 × 360_800k.mp4	30 fps	640 × 360 pixels	800 kbps
bbb_30fps_640 × 360_1000k.mp4	30 fps	640 × 360 pixels	1000 kbps
bbb_30fps_768 × 432_1500k.mp4	30 fps	768 × 432 pixels	1500 kbps
bbb_30fps_1024 × 576_2500k.mp4	30 fps	1024 × 576 pixels	2500 kbps
bbb_30fps_1280 × 720_4000k.mp4	30 fps	1280 × 720 pixels	4000 kbps
bbb_30fps_1920 × 1080_8000k.mp4	30 fps	1920 × 1080 pixels	8000 kbps

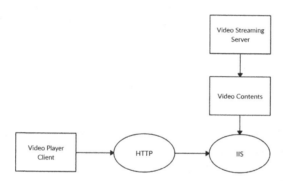

Fig. 9. Video streaming client-server model

The Video player clients in Fig. 9 run on hosts emulated by Mininet as shown in Fig. 8. The Mininet built on a computer installed Ubuntu Operating System version 18.04 64bit is used to emulate the simple and customized topology. To customize the bandwidth for each host-to-switch connection the TCLink library was used. There are 2 ways to control link bandwidth for a host in Mininet. The first one is to use Linux Traffic Control (qdisc) and the second method is to use TCLink library. Qdisc operates out of the Mininet, and it requires to shut down the link to assign new capability, then the link is turned on. In the latter, the control of the link bandwidth is easier because it is built-in in the Mininet.

4.2 Evaluate the Proposed Mechanism

The conducted experiment used the topology as illustrated in Fig. 8. The streaming was performed by the host h1, and file downloading was performed by the host h2. The bandwidth between the host h1 and the switch s1; the host h2 and the switch s1; the switch s1 and the server were all set to 10 Mbps.

To automate the experiment, a python program was developed to load Mininet environment with custom topology. The pseudocode of the python file is as follows:

```
Create a single switch topo
Create Mininet network
Add NAT technique to the network
Start the network
Get instance of hosts and switch
Set bandwidth to each link between host and switch
Start Command-Line interface of the network
```

Fig. 10. Pseudo code of creating emulated environment for the experiment

The procedure for this experiment is as follows:

Firstly, at the client-side, the python script described in Fig. 10 is used to start Mininet for network creation. At the same time, the bwm-ng tool is started to observe the receiving throughput over the network interface h1−eh0 of the host h1 and the network interface h2−eh0 of the host h2. Due to the simulation environment, we actually observe the network interface s1−eth1 and s1−eth2 of switch s1, which is directly connected to h1−eth0, h2−eth0, respectively.

On the server side, the video content has been placed in the web-server, waiting for request from video client. When a streaming session starts, its information will be captured by executing a shell script on the xterm terminal of the host h1.

When the monitoring module detects the first GET request with the maximum resolution of 1920 × 1080 pixels, which is the highest resolution available at the server, the file download is triggered. The file download information is also saved in a log file by executing a shell script on the xterm terminal of the host h2.

When the video segment is being downloaded, the bandwidth of file download is reduced so as not to affect the video stream. This was achieved by executing the following command:

```
py h2.connectionsTo(s1)[0][0].config(bw=1) , h2.connec-
tionsTo(s1)[0][1].config(bw=1), s1.cmd('sleep 4')
```

As shown in the command, the parameter bw is equal to 1 meaning that the bandwidth between h2 and s1 is going to be set to 1 Mbps. This bandwidth limitation only works for 4 s with the "sleep" command. During this time, the bandwidth of video streaming was 9 Mbps, which was sufficient for video quality not to be affected.

Once the video segment has been downloaded, the bandwidth for downloading the file is increased, the bandwidth for video streaming is reduced. This was achieved by executing the following command:

```
py h1.connectionsTo(s1)[0][0].config(bw=1) ,
h1.connectionsTo(s1)[0][1].config(bw=1) ,
h2.connectionsTo(s1)[0][0].config(bw=9) ,
h2.connectionsTo(s1)[0][1].config(bw=9), s1.cmd('sleep 9')
```

As shown in the command, bw = 1 means that the bandwidth between h1 and s1 was set to 1 Mbps; bw = 9 means that the bandwidth between h2 and s1 was set to 9 Mbps. This bandwidth limitation only works for 9 s with the "sleep" command. This is to make the video player not able to detect the bandwidth change.

Afterward, to prepare for the video client to make decision for the next GET request, the bandwidth for the video must be large enough so that there is no GET request with a lower resolution. For this purpose, the video bandwidth is increased, the bandwidth of the file download is reduced. This was achieved by executing the following command:

```
py h1.connectionsTo(s1)[0][0].config(bw=9) ,
h1.connectionsTo(s1)[0][1].config(bw=9) ,
h2.connectionsTo(s1)[0][0].config(bw=1) ,
h2.connectionsTo(s1)[0][1].config(bw=1)
```

This command adjusted the bandwidth between h1 and s1, the bandwidth between h2 and s1 to 9 Mbps and 1 Mbps, respectively. This returned enough bandwidth for h1 to have video with the highest quality.

The procedure was repeated 20 times. The obtained results show that the video quality was not reduced and the average file download duration was 15.5 s. Figures 11a and 11b compare the obtained results in three scenarios: A. Stable state, B. Bandwidth competition without our proposal, and C. Figure 11a shows that our proposed mechanism helps to maintain always the best video quality to the client even in case of bandwidth competition. Figure 11b shows that our proposed mechanism also helps the competitor application to have a faster connectivity than that when our mechanism is not applied. Specifically, the duration to download file was reduced more than ten percent from 17.29 s to 15.5 s.

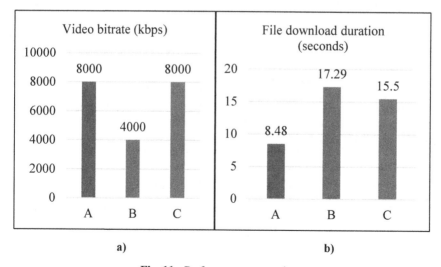

Fig. 11. Performance comparison

5 Conclusion

The goal of this work is to find a mechanism that guarantees the video quality and reduce the impact for the download file in case of bandwidth competition, has been achieved. The proposed mechanism has been implemented on a real testbed. The obtained results show that there is an 1.79-s improvement in reducing file download duration. This is about 10.35% as compared to the duration to download file in the bandwidth competition case. The important point is the quality of video streaming in the same experiment has been maintained.

In the future, this work will be extended to diverse scenarios where more clients participate in the network, more services compete for the bandwidth. Different types of video players and video streaming mechanisms will be explored. The control of the network will be executed from SDN controllers.

References

1. Akhshabi, S., Begen, A.C., Dovrolis, C.: An experimental evaluation of rate-adaptation algorithms in adaptive streaming over HTTP. In: Proceedings of the Second Annual ACM Conference on Multimedia Systems, pp. 157–168, February 2011
2. Nam, H., Kim, K.H., Calin, D., Schulzrinne, H.: Youslow: a performance analysis tool for adaptive bitrate video streaming. In: Proceedings of the 2014 ACM Conference on SIGCOMM, pp. 111–112, August 2014
3. Xu, X., Liu, J., Tao, X.: Mobile edge computing enhanced adaptive bitrate video delivery with joint cache and radio resource allocation. IEEE Access **5**, 16406–16415 (2017)
4. Bhat, D., Rizk, A., Zink, M., Steinmetz, R.: Network assisted content distribution for adaptive bitrate video streaming. In: Proceedings of the 8th ACM on Multimedia Systems Conference, pp. 62–75, June 2017
5. Georgopoulos, P., Elkhatib, Y., Broadbent, M., Mu, M., Race, N.: Towards network-wide QoE fairness using openflow-assisted adaptive video streaming. In: Proceedings of the 2013 ACM SIGCOMM Workshop on Future Human-Centric Multimedia Networking, pp. 15–20, August 2013
6. Bentaleb, A., Begen, A.C., Zimmermann, R.: SDNDASH: improving QoE of HTTP adaptive streaming using software defined networking. In: Proceedings of the 24th ACM International Conference on Multimedia, pp. 1296–1305, October 2016
7. Phan-Xuan, T., Kamioka, E.: Efficiency of QoE-driven network management in adaptive streaming over HTTP. In: 2016 22nd Asia-Pacific Conference on Communications (APCC), pp. 517–522. IEEE, August 2016
8. Lederer, S.: Optimal adaptive streaming formats MPEG-DASH & HLS Segment Length, Bitmovin Inc, 9 April 2015. https://bitmovin.com/mpeg-dash-hls-segment-length/
9. "Index of/129021/dash/akamai/bbb_30fps," DASH Industry Forum. http://dash.edgesuite.net/akamai/bbb_30fps/
10. "GPAC Nightly Builds," GPAC. https://gpac.wp.imt.fr/downloads/gpac-nightly-builds/

CNN-Based Book Cover and Back Cover Recognition and Classification

Haochang Xia, Yali Qi, Qingtao Zeng$^{(\boxtimes)}$, Yeli Li, and Fucheng You

Beijing Institute of Graphic Communication, Beijing, China
zengqingtao@bigc.edu.cn

Abstract. As an important part of the national economy and an important sup-porting industry, printing and publishing industry is closely related to the devel-opment of national economy. In recent years, the massive publication and printing of books has made the work of storing books in databases more and more onerous. The maturity of deep learning technology has brought good news to recognition and classification of books. Convolutional neural network is a good tool. Convo-lutional neural network is a technology in deep learning, often used in computer vision, image recognition classification and other fields. Research results in the field of book recognition and classification are relatively lacking. There is no good book data set that can be used for neural network training. In this paper, we col-lected a large number of book data sets and we built a set of image classification models based on CNN to identify and classify the cover and back cover of books. Through a lot of training and testing, we have generated a set of CNN models that can effectively identify and classify the cover and back cover of books. Compared with the traditional way of manually entering books into database, the use of neural networks makes the work more efficient and saves a lot of human resources.

Keywords: CNN · Deep learning · Image recognition · Image classification

1 Introduction

In recent years, artificial intelligence has developed rapidly, and machine learning has continued to make progress in the direction of image recognition and classification. In order to improve the accuracy of image recognition, many deep learning models have achieved good results, including: CNN, RNN, DBN, GAN, etc. Deep learning has achieved good results in the fields of face recognition and handwritten digit recognition. The initial idea was to use probably the best known of ML technologies; the convolutional neural network (CNN) which is used extensively for image recognition, particularly using the massive number of images available on the internet [1]. However, research in the fields of book recognition and classification is relatively lacking. In image processing field, CNNs can be used as an efficient and high-performance classification model and have gained outstanding performance [2].

This paper builds a set of image classification models based on the research of machine learning and neural network. First, we collected a large number of images of

© ICST Institute for Computer Sciences, Social Informatics and Telecommunications Engineering 2021
Published by Springer Nature Switzerland AG 2021. All Rights Reserved
Y. Weng et al. (Eds.): TridentCom 2020, LNICST 380, pp. 59–70, 2021.
https://doi.org/10.1007/978-3-030-77428-8_5

the cover and back cover of the book, and processed these images as a data set. Then build a set of neural networks, use these data sets to iteratively train and predict the neural network, and finally generate a training model that can effectively identify the book cover and back cover to achieve the classification effect.

2 Overview

With the development of Internet, the printing and publishing industry is also moving in the direction of digitization and networking. Among them, book digitization is an important area. The rapid development of machine learning and the rapid maturity of image recognition and classification technologies have greatly improved the efficiency of the book digital entry system. I have read a lot of literature and found that there are already many mature algorithms and image classification models in the field of computer vision and machine learning, however, there are still relatively few studies on applying these algorithms to the recognition and classification of book covers and back covers.

The identification and classification of books is a very heavy manual labor. On major online e-commerce platforms and university libraries, the traditional way of storing books to the database is to scan the barcodes code and obtain book pictures from the publisher. The traditional way has to upload the data manually. The use of machine learning technology to realize automatic recognition and classification of book covers, however, can reduce manual workload and improve work efficiency. On the other hand, it can also effectively improve the quality of classification and solve the problem that traditional manual scanning cannot identify the incomplete books.

3 Basic Principles of Deep Learning

3.1 Neural Networks

3.1.1 Neurons

The simplest neuron structure is a model that contains data input, result output, and corresponding calculation methods. The data is passed in by the input neuron. According to the weight of each input neuron, the sum is calculated by weight, and then the result is passed to the activation function for processing. Finally, the output data is obtained by this way. In the formula, letter w represents the weight, and letter x stands for data input. As we can see, different inputs get different weight. The letter b represents a constant parameter, and y(x) represents neuron calculation results.

The calculation formula of neuron is shown as follows:

$$y(x) = f(l + b) = f\left(\sum_{i=1}^{n} w_i x_i + b\right) \tag{1}$$

3.1.2 Multilayer Neural Network

In order to cope with a more complex environment, in practical applications, a multilayer neural network structure is generally used. This neural network structure is also called feedforward neural network. Its first layer is called the input layer, the middle layer is called the hidden layer, the hidden layer can contain multiple layers of neuron structure, and the last layer is called the output layer. The neurons in the upper layer and the neurons in the next layer are connected by means of full connections. Neurons that are not in the same layer do not communicate, and neurons in the same layer are independent of each other. Data is transferred from the input layer to the hidden layer, and the hidden layer is solved layer by layer through corresponding calculation methods, we get the output until the last layer is calculated. Figure 1 shows the general multi-layer neural network.

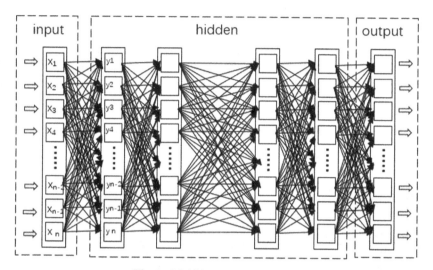

Fig. 1. Multi-layer neural network

3.2 Convolutional Neural Network

3.2.1 Convolutional Layer

Convolutional layer is the structure used for feature extraction in CNN. The convolutional layer applies several filters to the input data to perform operations. The filter is an operation in image processing. The specific operation of filtering is the sum of the product of the image pixels and the filter [3]. Here, the filters are called convolution kernels. Each part of the information is extracted through the convolution kernel, and the feature information is re-integrated through weight sharing to obtain a new feature map. The pixel value on the picture and the convolution kernel are multiplied and summed correspondingly to obtain a new feature value. Calculation process of the convolution operation is shown in the Fig. 2.

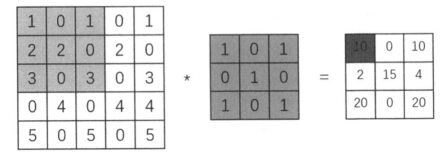

Fig. 2. The calculation process of the convolution operation

3.2.2 Pooling Layer

The pooling layer takes the down-samples for input feature map. This method can reduce the size of the feature map, thereby reducing the amount of calculation, and can also increase the translation robustness to the certain extent. Generally speaking, there are two forms of pooling layer: maximum pooling and average pooling. The maximum pooling method is to take the maximum value of the feature points in the window neighborhood, and the average pooling method is to take the average of the feature points in the window neighborhood. The two pooling methods of maximum pooling and average pooling are shown in the Fig. 3.

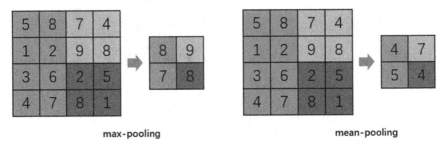

max-pooling   mean-pooling

Fig. 3. Maximum pooling and average pooling

3.2.3 Activation Function

In a neural network, if there is only a convolutional layer, the relationship between input and output is just a simple linear operation. The input data x is processed by the activation function, and a new result is obtained, which improves the expressive ability of the linear model. In order to make the neural network better fit the nonlinear problem, but also help to make the deep neural network really work, it is necessary to use the nonlinear activation function. Commonly used activation functions include the following.

(1) The Sigmoid function, also known as the Logistic function, is the most widely used activation function in the early days. The mathematical expression is as follows:

$$Sigmoid(x) = \frac{1}{1 + e^{-x}} \quad (2)$$

The output range of the Sigmoid function is in the (0,1) interval, and it grows continuously and monotonously, which can be well applied to classification problems.

(2) Tanh function, also known as hyperbolic tangent function, its shape is similar to sigmoid, and its mathematical expression is as follows:

$$\tanh(x) = \frac{e^x - e^{-x}}{e^x + e^{-x}} \quad (3)$$

The output value of the Tanh function is between [-1,1]. Like the Sigmoid function, there is also a saturation problem. The Tanh function can be seen as two Sigmoid functions. When the input value of the function is less than zero, the output value is less than zero, when it is equal to zero, the output value is equal to zero, and when it is greater than zero, the output value is greater than zero.

(3) The rectified linear unit (ReLU) function is the most used activation function in practical applications. Its mathematical expression is as follows:

$$f(x) = \begin{cases} 0, x < 0 \\ x, x \geq 0 \end{cases} \quad (4)$$

The expression of the ReLU function is very simple, but it works very well. Whether it is forward propagation or back propagation, the amount of calculation is very small and the training process is fast.

3.2.4 Fully Connected Layer

The processes of convolution, pooling, and activation in the neural network belong to the feature extraction stage of the image, and only the final fully connected layer accomplishes the classification task. The specific method is to map the feature space to the sample label space.

The fully connected layer performs weighted summation and offset operations on the input values. All values in the vector are weighted and summed with the weights corresponding to each convolution kernel to obtain the characteristic response. The number of characteristic responses is determined by the number of cores in the fully connected layer. The fully connected layer increases the complexity of the model, and theoretically improves the generalization ability of the model.

As shown in Fig. 1, the connection between the first input layer and the hidden layer is full connection. If the input layer has only three parameters, and the first hidden layer also has three output parameters. A simpler hierarchy like this, the calculation formula between them can be expressed as:

$$\begin{pmatrix} y1 \\ y2 \\ y3 \end{pmatrix} = \begin{pmatrix} W_{11} & W_{12} & W_{13} \\ W_{21} & W_{22} & W_{23} \\ W_{31} & W_{32} & W_{33} \end{pmatrix} * \begin{pmatrix} x1 \\ x2 \\ x3 \end{pmatrix} + \begin{pmatrix} b1 \\ b2 \\ b3 \end{pmatrix} \quad (5)$$

3.2.5 Error Back Propagation

The training process of convolutional neural network is divided into two stages. The first stage is the forward propagation, which transforms the propagation of data from low-level to high-level. The neural network calculates and stores the intermediate variables of the model layer by layer in the order from the input layer to the output layer. The second stage is the back propagation. When the output result of the forward propagation does not match the expectation, the error is propagated and trained from the high-level to the bottom-level. According to the order from the output layer to the input layer, the objective function is calculated and stored layer by layer. The intermediate variables of the segment and the gradient of the parameters are modified in turn to modify the parameter values between the connections of each layer. The modification of the parameter values is determined by the error of the back-end data input.

4 Image Recognition Classification Model Based on CNN

4.1 Experimental Environment

The experiment uses Python and PyTorch development environment for programming and model training. As we know, Python is one of the most popular computer programming languages in the field of machine learning. It has a rich standard library and a strong third-party ecosystem. PyTorch is a python-based scientific computing package. It can be used as a substitute for NumPy, it uses the powerful performance of GPU for calculations, or as a highly flexible and fast deep learning platform. PyTorch is an optimized tensor library for deep learning using GPUs and CPUs. PyTorch provides the elegantly designed modules and classes torch.nn, torch.optim, Dataset, and Data Loader to help you create and train neural networks.

4.2 Data Preprocessing

4.2.1 Data Set

For each CNN model, a "multi-scale summation" module is employed to avoid overfitting that is usually caused by limited training data [4]. The recognition accuracy of the image classification model largely depends on the quality of the data set. For the design of neural network recognition system, it is very important to have a sufficient amount of labeled training data, and the data contains as many complex environmental changes as possible. The data set used in this article mainly comes from the two major e-commerce platforms of JD.com and Dangdang.com. Table 1 shows the specific categories of the data set.

4.2.2 Data Set Processing

The data set collected 3,600 images containing book cover and back cover from online shopping malls (JD.com and Dangdang.com). These book images have three different kinds of environments, including main-picture scene, multi-picture scene, and publishing

Table 1. Book cover and back cover data set.

Data sources	Category	Number
JD.com	Cover	900
JD.com	Back cover	900
Dangdang.com	Cover	900
Dangdang.com	Back cover	900

house scene. The main-picture scene is a single cover or back cover picture; the multi-picture scene is a picture that may contain more than one book; the publishing house scene is the cover or back cover of the book containing the content information recommended by the publisher. In view of the daily actual use, the cover and back cover images of the book are randomly selected from the three scenes at a ratio of 1:1:1 to build a training set. The number of images in the test set depends on the actual situation.

In consideration of the working mechanism of the convolutional neural network, we need to preprocess the images due to the different sizes of the collected data sets. In order to facilitate the operation of convolution operation, while keeping the basic information of the original image as much as possible, the cropping method is to first scale the image proportionally, so as to preserve the original image content to the greatest extent, and then perform center cropping to make the training data more accurate. All this operation is to make sure that the input image contains the complete central information of the original image.

4.3 Design and Construction of Neural Network Model

4.3.1 CNN (Convolutional Neural Network)

In deep learning, convolutional neural network is a special deep neural network, often used in the field of computer vision. CNN is composed of input layer, convolution layer, activation function, pooling layer, and fully connected layer. The most prominent advantage of CNN is high-speed parallel computing and processing speed not influenced by the size of image, so it is convenient for hardware implementation [5].

In the convolutional neural network, the input layer refers to the input image data, which is generally stored in the form of a matrix. The data set we collected contains pictures of various sizes. To facilitate the calculation, we processed the training set and unified the size of the training set pictures to 200 * 200 pixels.

In the convolution process, the convolution kernel extracts image features by convolution calculation operations on the input layer image. When building the neural network, we used two convolutional layers here.

The activation function is a processing function added to fit the input-output relationship of nonlinear characteristics. In CNN, each convolution operation process of the convolution kernel is to sum up the products of various positions in the template, input the accumulated value into the activation function, and then use the output value as the convolution result. This paper uses the ReLU function as the activation function of the experiment.

The pooling layer compresses the input feature map to make the feature map smaller and simplify the computational complexity of the neural network; on the other hand, the main purpose of feature compression is to extract the main features. Corresponding to the two-layer convolutional layer, we use a two-layer pooling layer, and the method used by the pooling layer is maximum pooling.

The fully connected layer contains input nodes and output nodes. The input nodes receive the output data of the previous layer, after calculation, the result is passed to the output nodes, and the output nodes transmits the data to the next layer of the neural network, thereby passing the output value to the classifier. Usually the result of CNN n-class classifier models is obtained with the selection of the maximum among the n output nodes of the final fully-connected layer [6]. This paper uses three fully connected layers, and finally two output results are obtained, corresponding to the probability values of the book cover and back cover. The Fig. 4 below shows the CNN model built in this paper.

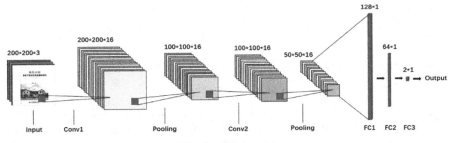

Fig. 4. CNN model

4.3.2 Building a Convolutional Neural Network

The deep neural network constructed in this paper contains a multi-layer structure, where the image size of the input layer is 200*200 pixels, and the image here has been processed in the data set preprocessing stage. In addition, the neural network constructed in this paper includes two convolutional layers, two pooling layers and three fully connected layers. The structure of the convolutional neural network is shown in Table 2.

Table 2. The CNN structure of the book cover and back cover classification.

Layer	Depth	Number	Size
Input layer	3	–	200 × 200
Convolution layer 1	3	16	3 × 3
Pooling layer 1	–	–	2 × 2
Convolution layer 2	16	16	3 × 3
Pooling layer 2	–	–	2 × 2
Fully connected layer 1	–	–	40000(in) 128(out)
Fully connected layer 2	–	–	128(in) 64(out)
Fully connected layer 3	–	–	64(in) 2(out)

4.4 Model Training

Model training is divided into several stages. First, the input layer obtains the processed 24-bit jpg format RGB three-channel image. After the first convolution operation, the output image is a 16-channel 200 * 200 pixels image. Then we perform the first pooling operation. The pooling layer uses a 2 * 2 Max Pooling and outputs a 100 * 100 * 16 matrix. Next it is the second convolution operation, after that we can obtain a new matrix of 100*100*16.

After all this, it is the second pooling operation, the image is reduced to 50 * 50 at this time. At last, we have three full connections options, and the input nodes here are separately 40,000, 128, and 64. The number of output nodes of the last one is 2. These two nodes correspond to two output values, including the probability of the book cover and back cover. Figure 5 shows the recognition result.

This paper provides a convolutional neural network model built on the pytorch framework. Pytorch offers a rich API interface for the construction of deep neural networks. At the same time, it takes full advantage of the good computing speed of the GPU. Selecting the pytorch framework to use the GPU for calculations saves a lot of time for model training and testing. The experimental operating system is Windows 10, and the experimental environment is Intel Core i7-9750H CPU and NVIDIA GeForce GTX 1660Ti GPU.

5 Model Assessment

In the experiment, different training times and learning rates were set for the constructed model to observe the experimental data. For each CNN model, a "multi-scale summation" module is employed to avoid overfitting that is usually caused by limited training data [4]. In order to improve the classification effect of the convolutional neural network model and achieve good predictions on new data, the data set is divided into three subsets (training set, validation set and test set). Because the data set is relatively scarce, it can't cope with all situations. But we can simulate more training data by increasing the number of training. A too high learning rate will increase the risk of overfitting, and a too low

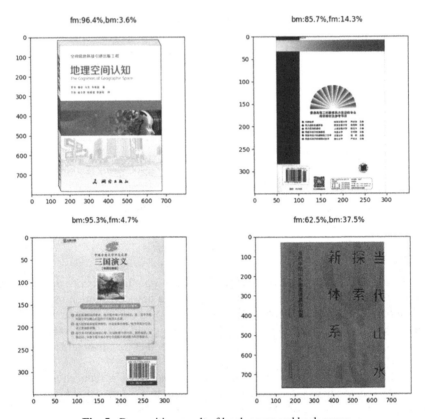

Fig. 5. Recognition result of book cover and back cover

learning rate combined with relatively scarce training data may cause the learning model to fail to learn specific feature values. Part of the training data is shown in Table 3.

It can be seen from the experimental data that when the number of training rounds is 3 and the learning rate is 0.001, the accuracy of the test reaches the highest. When the number of training rounds is 5, the accuracy rate reaches the highest and the learning rate is 0.001 as well. With the same number of training rounds, it seems that the accuracy of the model decreases as the learning rate increases. However, when the number of training rounds is adjusted to 10 rounds, the highest point of the accuracy of the model falls in the case of the lowest learning rate at 0.0001. After constant adjustment and testing of the parameters, we finally set the number of training rounds to 20 rounds and the learning rate of 0.01 as the final parameters of our model, and the test results are good, with an accuracy of 97.6%. In the future work, we will investigate many supervised learning algorithms such as: SVM [7], k-nearest neighbors [8] and Boosted Regression Trees [9, 10] to classify an image. If I combine multiple machine learning methods, the accuracy will be further improved.

Table 3. Training data

Train number	Epoch	Learning rate	Test accuracy
1	3	0.0001	0.5799476
2	3	0.001	0.7421927
3	3	0.01	0.5049149
4	5	0.0001	0.7311714
5	5	0.001	0.9067465
6	5	0.01	0.5064889
7	10	0.0001	0.93220395
8	10	0.001	0.8237559
9	10	0.01	0.5196011
10	20	0.0001	0.9116753
11	20	0.001	0.9758636
12	20	0.01	0.50095326

6 Conclusion

Machine learning (ML) is an algorithm set especially suited to prediction. These ML methods are easier to implement and perform better than the classical statistical approaches [11]. This paper builds a set of convolutional neural networks through the research of deep learning to identify and classify the cover and back cover of books. By revising the different parameters in the construction model, a relatively good accuracy rate has been achieved, which provides a certain reference for book identification and classification. Due to the limited ability of the author, I failed to provide a more perfect solution for book classification. Machine learning is often inseparable from big data. My next step is to improve the book classification data set and classify the data set according to book categories. Through these works, we can provide various special diagnosis attributes for the training of neural networks to adapt to various complex situations. At the same time, we can optimize algorithms and modify models to improve recognition accuracy.

Acknowlegments. 1. Beijing science and technology innovation service capability construction project (PXM2016_014223_000025).

2. Major special project of science and technology of Guangdong Province, No: 190826175545233.

3. BIGC Project (Ec202007).

References

1. Padfield, N.: Exploring the classification of acoustic transients with machine learning. In: Proceedings of ACOUSTICS 2019, vol. 10, no. 13 (2019)

2. Leng, J., Li, T., Bai, G., et al.: Cube-CNN-SVM: a novel hyperspectral image classification method. In: 2016 IEEE 28th International Conference on Tools with Artificial Intelligence (ICTAI), pp. 1027–1034. IEEE (2016)
3. Yin, Q., Zhang, R., Shao, X.L.: CNN and RNN mixed model for image classification. In: MATEC Web of Conferences. EDP Sciences, vol. 277, p. 02001 (2019)
4. Zhang, M., Li, W., Du, Q.: Diverse region-based CNN for hyperspectral image classification. IEEE Trans. Image Process. 27(6), 2623–2634 (2018)
5. Qingling, J.: Edge detection for color image based on CNN. Int. J. Adv. Inf. Sci. Serv. Sci. 3(10), 61–69 (2011)
6. Jhang, K.: Gender prediction based on voting of CNN models. In: 2019 International Conference on Green and Human Information Technology (ICGHIT), pp. 89–92. IEEE (2019)
7. Piyush, R.: Hyperplane based classification: perceptron and (Intro to) support vector machines. In: CS5350/6350: Machine Learning (2011)
8. Domeniconi, C., Gunopulos, D., Peng, J.: Large margin nearest neighbor classifiers. IEEE Trans. Neural Netw. 16(4), 899–909 (2005)
9. Rokach, L., Maimon, O.: Data mining with decision trees: theory and applications. World Scientific Pub Co Inc. (2008). ISBN: 978-9812771711
10. Friedman, J.H.: Greedy function approximation: a gradient boosting machine (1999)
11. Breiman, L.: Statistical modeling: the two cultures. Stat. Sci. 16, 199–215 (2001)

A Case Study of Linguistic Research Methods in the Age of Computing

TieJun Shao[1,3,4]([✉]), JianShe Zhou[1,3], and WenYan Zhang[2]

[1] Capital Normal University, Beijing, China
2180101027@cnu.edu.cn
[2] China Fire and Rescue Institute, Beijing, China
[3] Research Center for Language Intelligence of China, Beijing, China
[4] North China Institute of Science and Technology, Beijing, China

Abstract. With the development of technologies such as computers, Artificial Intelligence, and Big Data new research methods have emerged in the traditional social sciences. With the help of new research methods, the efficiency and accuracy of quantitative analysis can be improved, which helps to improve research efficiency and demonstrate research trends. This paper uses the data analysis software CiteSpace as an example to analyze the current research situation of domestic Tibetan-Burman Language research, and graphically display the analysis results.

Keywords: Artificial intelligence · Bibliometric analysis · CiteSpace

1 Introduction

With the development of technologies such as computers, Artificial Intelligence, and Big Data, new research methods have emerged in the traditional social sciences. With the help of new research methods, the efficiency and accuracy of quantitative analysis can be improved, which is helpful to improve research efficiency and display research trends. Linguistics is the subject of human language research. The scope of exploration includes the nature, function, structure, application and historical development of language, as well as other language-related issues. The object of linguistic research is objectively existing language facts. Whether it is modern language or ancient language, it is an objective language phenomenon.

In China, due to historical, geographic and other factors, ethnic minority languages are an integral part of linguistic research. Tibeto-Burman language is the language family with the widest distribution, the largest internal differences in the Sino-Tibetan language family. The Tibetan-Burman languages in China are mainly distributed in Tibet, Gansu, Yunnan, Sichuan, Guizhou, Guangxi, Hunan, Hubei and other provinces and autonomous regions. Tibeto-Burman language is an important content in linguistic research, and it has special value for the construction of linguistic theory and national culture research. The comparative study of Tibeto-Burman language in China started relatively late, but the study of Tibeto-Burman language has developed from the original research interest of a

Y. Weng et al. (Eds.): TridentCom 2020, LNICST 380, pp. 71–79, 2021.
https://doi.org/10.1007/978-3-030-77428-8_6

few scholars to an important branch of current linguistics. Through the efforts of several generations, Tibetan-Burman language research has achieved considerable results. In the face of vigorous Tibetan-Burman language research, we must not only think about what results have been obtained in Tibetan-Burman language research, which aspects have been sufficiently studied, and which aspects are still available. Very weak, how can we make greater breakthroughs in Tibetan-Burman language research? Therefore, this article uses the Tibetan-Burman language research from 1992 to 2019 as the data source, and uses the visualization function of the Citespace software to quantitatively analyze the development status and trends of Tibetan-Burman language research.

1.1 Research Method

Bibliometric analysis is to use mathematical and statistical methods to quantitatively analyze a given knowledge carrier. Through a quantitative analysis of literature in a certain field, basic information such as research overview, research hotspots, and research distribution in the field can be obtained. This information has a good reference value for researchers to sort out the research context of the field and discover the research innovation points in the field. CiteSpace is a visual bibliometric analysis software developed by the team of information visualization expert Chen Chaomei. This software can perform keyword clustering analysis of scientific literature, author cooperation network analysis, etc., and display the analysis results in visual forms such as timeline and knowledge structure map. At present, few scholars use professional tool software to carry out bibliometric analysis of Tibetan-Burman language research. This article combines the needs of Tibetan-Burman language research and the characteristics of CiteSpace's visualization tools, and uses CiteSpace to do quantitative analysis and visual display of Tibetan-Burman literature.

1.2 Research Data Sources

The object of quantitative analysis in this article is related papers on Tibetan-Burman language research. The research data comes from CNKI database of CNKI. The search condition is "topic = Tibetan-Burman", the source category is "core journals", and the retrieval time is April 2020. On the 27th, a total of 425 documents with the theme of "Tibetan-Burman" were retrieved, and the time span was from 1992 to 2019. Since this article conducts statistical analysis on Tibetan-Burman language research on a yearly basis, 2020 has not yet ended, so the time span ends in 2019 to facilitate statistics throughout the year. In order to ensure the accuracy of the retrieved literature data, the retrieval results were manually screened before analysis, and related seminars, linguistic conferences, person news, seminar reviews, and published information were deleted to obtain a total of 376 documents that were effectively.

2 Analysis of Annual Paper Volume

This article counts the papers on the Tibetan-Burman language in the core journals of CNKI from 1992 to 2019, and analyzes the annual number of papers in this field.

The annual volume of papers is one of the important indicators to measure the development of a certain research field. To a certain extent, it can reflect the improvement of knowledge in the field, the research progress of researchers, and the popularity of field research. Figure 1 shows the distribution of the number of articles issued in the Tibetan-Burman language research field from 1992 to 2019. From the figure, it can be seen that the core amount of articles issued in the Tibetan-Burman language research field in China is a research trend that tends to be stable while changing., The average annual number of articles published is 13.5.

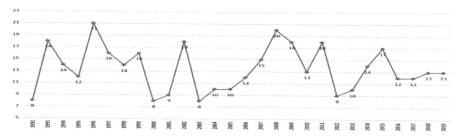

Fig. 1. Annual paper volume from 1992–2019.

From 1992 to 2015, the number of publications in Tibeto-Burman language research was wavy, and there were several peaks and valleys in the number of publications. Among them, the number of publications increased year by year from 2005 to 2008, indicating that the study of Tibeto-Burman language in China during this period is relatively hot, new research hotspots have emerged, knowledge has been improved more, and more research results have been published. Language contact, cross-language comparison, and linguistic issues related to the Tibetan-Yi Corridor are all research hotspots in this period; the research content involves specific issues such as language family issues, phonetics, vocabulary, and grammar, such as "Some Thoughts on Grammar Comparison", "Language Contact and Cultural Diffusion on the Silk Road", etc., the research field covers a wide range and rich results.

After 2008, Tibetan-Burman language research has experienced a fluctuating decline. From 2016 to 2019, the number of publications has been steadily changing, but the annual publication volume of 2016–2019 is lower than the average annual publication volume of the 1992–2019 interval. The changes in the number of articles published every year indicate that there is still a large research space in the Tibetan-Burman language research field on the basis of existing subjects, and there is the potential for new research hotspots.

3   Source Journal Analysis

Professional academic journals are the main carrier for the release of subject research results, an important platform for subject exchanges, and the main medium for researchers to obtain research materials and understand academic frontiers. The ability of research results to be published in professional journals also recognizes the academic level of scholars. The chart of journals containing Tibetan-Burman research papers from

1992 to 2019 and the number of collections. Through statistics and analysis of domestic journals containing Tibetan-Burman research papers, it is not difficult to find that the journal with the largest number of Tibetan-Burman research papers is " National Language and Language Studies. During the statistical period, "Ethnic Language" published a total of 144 papers on Tibetan and Burmese, and "Language Studies" published a total of 50 papers, accounting for 38.3% and 13.3% of the number of statistical papers. The total issue of the two journals The number of publications accounted for 51.6% of the number of statistical papers, that is, more than 50% of the Tibetan-Burman language research papers were published in "Ethnic Languages" and "Language Studies" during the statistical period.

"National Language" was founded in 1979 and is sponsored by the Institute of Ethnology and Anthropology of the Chinese Academy of Social Sciences. The journal focuses on the facts of various Chinese languages as the main research object. It is based on Sino-Tibetan, Altaic, South Asian and Austronesian languages. The publication is the main research object. "Language Studies" was founded in 1981 and sponsored by the Institute of Chinese Languages of Huazhong University of Science and Technology. The journal focuses on various languages in China as its research objects. The content includes the exploration of linguistic theoretical methods and the evaluation of new theories, Chinese and minority languages And the description of dialects, the historical comparative study of relative languages, etc.

Due to the different positioning and focus of the journal, the focus of the Tibetan-Burman essays published in National Language and Language Studies is also different. The Tibetan-Burman essays published in "Ethnic Languages" pay more attention to specific ethnic languages, language homologous relations and other issues, placing the study of Tibetan-Burman languages within the framework of minority languages, such as "Liangshan Yi Tone and Expressions", "Innovation and Division of Rong Language Branch", "Phonetic Features and Variations of Zhuang Language in Yunnan Ninglang", "Range and Range of Word Choices in Comparison of Cognate Words Standards—Take the formulation of the comparison table of Tibetan-Burman cognate words as an example" and "The Distribution and Sources of Tibetan-Burmese Words", etc.; Tibetan-Burman papers published in "Language Studies" more Pay attention to the language itself, and conduct research from the perspectives of language types, phonetics, and grammar, such as "The Territorial Structure of Tibeto-Burman Language in Southeast Tibet", "The Yinsheng Vowel System of Miao-Yao Language", "Bisu Language Status and Significance in Historical Comparison", "Types and Characteristics of Africatives in Ethnic Languages of Southern China", etc.

Domestic research on Tibeto-Burman language is not only limited to linguistic studies, but also involves the study of ethnic minorities in the southwest. Therefore, some relevant research papers on Tibeto-Burman language are also published in journals such as Guizhou Ethnic Studies and Ideological Front, such as Huang Lihong Published in "Guizhou Ethnic Studies", "The Historical Textual Research of my country's Tibetan-Burman Ethnic Minorities Migrating Southward", etc. It can be seen that academic papers on Tibetan-Burman language studies are mainly published in academic journals related to linguistics and ethnology.

4 Keyword Analysis

4.1 Keyword Co-occurrence Analysis

Keywords are used to express the main content of the article. The keywords can reflect the main research results of the article. CiteSpace is used to analyze the keywords of the literature. The distribution of high-frequency keywords in the research field can be seen through intuitive visualization, so as to understand the corresponding Research hotspots.

The high-frequency keywords mainly include: Tibeto-Burman, Sino-Tibetan, Tibeto-Burman, Sino-Tibetan, Yi branch, Dong-Taiwan, historical comparison, prefix, vowels, etc. Since this article is a literature search on the subject of "Tibetan-Burman", it is not meaningful to analyze the high-frequency words Tibetan-Burman separately, so it mainly analyzes other high-frequency words. Table 1 shows the top 15 keywords of frequency.

Table 1. Words with high-frequency.

No	Frequency	Word
1	127	Tibetan Burmese Language
2	46	Sino Tibetan language family
3	32	Tibeto-Burman Branch
4	28	Dong Tai language
5	24	Yi language branch
6	23	Chinese Tibetan
7	19	Historical comparison
8	16	Construction
9	14	Prefix
10	14	Initial consonant
11	14	chinese
12	14	Personal pronouns
13	13	Three body pronouns
14	12	Miao-Yao
15	11	Voice

From the above frequency table, it is not difficult to see the relationship between the Tibetan-Burman, Chinese and Sino-Tibetan language families, as well as the specific research content involved in the Tibetan-Burman language research. The high-frequency keywords obtained through CiteSpace analysis belong to the scope of Tibetan-Burman language research, and can also directly reflect the characteristics and key issues of the current Tibetan-Burman language research, such as the Dong-Tai language, Yi branch, structure, prefix shown in Table 1. Initials, phonetics, etc. These are the hotspots of current research, and it also reflects that the current Tibetan-Burman language research focuses on phonetics, which is consistent with the characteristics of most languages of the Tibetan-Burman language that only have phonetics without text. On the other hand, it can be seen that the current Tibetan-Burman grammar and vocabulary research is relatively small, and there is still much room for research in this area in the future.

Co-occurring words that appeared earlier include Sino-Tibetan, Sino-Tibetan language family, historical comparison, construction, affix (1993), Burmese branch, Dong-Taiwan, phonetic (1997), vocabulary comparison, cognate characters, Ancient Sounds (1998), Thai, Siamese (1999); Co-occurring words that appeared later include Bai (2010), historical typology, typology (2011), copula, judgment word (2013) etc. Through the temporal changes of keyword co-occurrence, we can summarize the brief evolutionary context of the study of Tibeto-Burman language in my country. In the early stage of the study, the study focused on specific language from the perspectives of word formation and phonetics. Based on these studies, it began to appear in the later period. Linguistics and typology study the integrity of Tibeto-Burman language. It reflects the evolution of Tibetan-Burman language research from concrete to abstract, from individuality to generality, from linguistic data investigation to the establishment of disciplinary research framework.

Summarizing the evolution of Tibetan-Burman language research is to start with a specific research problem of a single language in the early stage of the research, such as word prefixes and suffix issues, and then use historical comparison to analyze the relationship between languages in the Tibetan-Burman language family from the perspective of morphology. The evolution relationship is analyzed. With the increase of research materials and the advancement of research theories, typological theories are used to conduct more in-depth research on Tibetan-Burman language.

4.2 Keyword Cluster Analysis

Using CiteSpace to perform clustering analysis on co-occurring keywords can get research hotspots in the research field. This paper uses the LSI clustering algorithm provided by Cite Space to cluster high-frequency co-occurring words in Tibetan and Burmese, a total of 7 cluster labels are obtained, namely #0 Tujia language, #1 morphology (grammar), #2 Tibetan, #3 root, #4 tone system, #5 series and #6 Dong Dai language family. These key The clustering of words can reflect the research hotspots of Tibeto-Burman in China.

#0Tujia Language Cluster. The main content includes Tujia language, pure four-class rhyme, Yi language, ethnic linguistics, historical typology, Daofu language, Muya language, comparative research, ethnic minorities, folk literature, language investigation, open syllables, Continuous tone sandhi, inflection, Li Fanggui, ethnology, language branch, Bai nationality, etc. This clustering shows that the current research on Tujia language is mainly focused on phonetics, and compared with other languages, the characteristics of the phonetics are obtained to explore the family of Tujia language.

#1 Morphology (Grammar). The main content of clustering includes morphology (grammar), person, pronunciation, polyphony, imperative, vowel, pre-addition, attribute,

Burmese, ancient Chinese, consistent relationship, post-addition, rhyme ending, Tones, Burmese branch, etc. This clustering fully shows how the morphology changes and its effects.

#2 The Main Content of Tibetan. Clustering includes Tibetan, sayings, Siamese, Miao-Yao, Zhuang-Dai, Dong-Taiwan, Thai, Dong, Dong-Shui, ancient sounds, phonetics, cognate characters, Alternate relations, Shui language, dialectology, Jingpo language, Chinese dialects, Sino-Tibetan, primitive Sino-Tibetan, Tibeto-Burman language family, trishen pronouns, vowels, phonetics, personal pronouns, etc. There are many keywords in this cluster, which reflects the depth of Tibetan language research so far, and also reflects the important role and significance of Tibetan language in Tibetan-Burman language research.

#3 The Main Content of Root Clustering. Includes roots, associated markers, morphemes, cognates, Shang and Zhou dynasties, causal complex sentences, underlying words, Zhou Dynasty, hypothetical sentences, common words, correspondence, verb overlap, methodological issues, and imitation of ancient, Tibetan language, Chinese studies, verb overlap, etc. This clustering reflects scholars' tracing of roots, the relationship between roots and cognates, and the important role of roots in language research.

#4 Tone System Clustering. Mainly includes tone system, grammatical category, typology, Tibeto-Burman language, Dong Dai language family, balance state, Zhuang Dong language family, language typology, causative usage, directional verbs, grammar, syntactic format, language Groups, linguistic commonalities, Yin tones, Jianyu style, phase space, intransitiveness, tones, order, Qiang branch, suffix, language system, continuum, modern Chinese, etc. Tone is an important feature of Chinese-Tibetan languages in phonetics. This clustering reflects the extensiveness of tonal research and the involvement of new theories and new perspectives, such as equilibrium and phase space.

#5 Cohort Clustering. Mainly includes copulas, judgment words, historical comparison, interpretive sentences, demonstrative pronouns, conceptual structure, verbal characteristics, judgment sentences, difference, construction, first person, Tibetan branch, Sino-Tibetan Department etc. This clustering can see the role and significance of copulas in the field of research.

#6 The Main Content of Dong Dai Language. Cluster includes Dong Dai language family, equilibrium, cognate words, Zhuang-Dong language family, three-shen pronouns, tones, roots, Bai language, etc.

It can be seen that cluster analysis can provide intuitive and visual research focus and direction. Facilitating the extraction and processing of key information is conducive to our grasp of research directions and research hotspots.

4.3 Keyword Evolution Trend Analysis

CiteSpcae provides a knowledge graph displayed in a time zone view (Timezone View). The time zone view displays the changes of keywords in the field literature from the time dimension. At the same time, you can intuitively understand the number of keywords in the current year through the distribution of nodes and lines in the corresponding year, that is, more lines indicate high There are more frequent keywords. It can be seen from the figure that there were no high-frequency keywords in 2003–2006 and 2014–2019. Combined with the analysis of the number of publications in 2.1 years, the annual publication volume of these two time periods was continuously lower than the annual average publication volume, that is, the study of Tibetan-Burman There are no major research hotspots in the field, and the output of research results is small.

5   Conclusion

This paper uses the bibliometric software CiteSpace to conduct a simple quantitative analysis of the domestic Tibetan-Burmese research field. The analysis includes the author, the publishing organization, and the co-occurrence of keywords. The conclusions are drawn as follow:

(1)   New research methods such as computers, artificial intelligence, and big data can improve the efficiency and accuracy of quantitative analysis, help improve research efficiency and show research trends.
(2)   The cooperation mode is single. Most of the authors in the field of Tibetan-Burman language research in China are independent researches and articles, and the existing cooperative relationships are mostly teachers or colleagues. Although this kind of cooperation has cultivated new forces for Tibetan-Burman language research, it is at the same time Lack of research and cooperation within the field and across fields, and there are certain limitations in research methods and research theories, which is not conducive to the creation of academic innovations;
(3)   There is currently a lack of new research hotspots in the Tibetan-Burman language field, and there have been few Tibetan-Burman research papers in recent years;
(4)   (Research methods lack innovation. The existing Tibetan-Burman language research is mostly based on traditional linguistic research methods, and there is no combination of information and intelligent research methods in the Internet age.

Acknowledgement. This research was financially supported by "Research on key technologies and model verification of prose genre oriented text understanding (ZDI135-101)", "Research and Application of Key Technologies of Intelligent Auxiliary Reading System (ZDI135-79)",Capacity Building for Sci-Tech Innovation-Fundamental Scientific Research Foundation (20530290082).

References

1.   Yang, H., Shao, X.X., Wu, M.: A review on ecosystem health research: a visualization based on CiteSpace. Sustainability **11**, 4908 (2019)
2.   Zheng, K.Y., Wang, X.Q.: Publications on the association between cognitive function and pain from 2000 to 2018: a bibliometric analysis using CiteSpace. Med. Sci. Monitor. **25**, 8940–8951 (2019)

3. Moher, D., Liberati, A., Tetzlaff, J., Altman, D.G.: Preferred reporting items for systematic reviews and meta-analyses: the PRISMA statement. Ann. Int. Med. **151**, 264–269 (2009)
4. Yao, Q., et al.: Scientometric trends and knowledge maps of global health systems research. Health Res. Policy Syst. **12** (2014)
5. Archambault, E., Campbell, D., Gingras, Y., Lariviere, V.: Comparing of science bibliometric statistics obtained from the web and scopus. J. Am. Soc. Inf. Sci. Technol. **60**, 1320–1326 (2009)
6. Hou, J.H., Yang, X.C., Chen, C.M.: Emerging trends and new developments in information science: a document co-citation analysis (2009–2016). Scientometrics **115**, 869–892 (2018)
7. Martin, D.J., Simon, J., Daan, S., Zhan, C.J., Margot, W.: Sustainable-smart-resilient-low carbon-eco-knowledge cities; making sense of a multitude of concepts promoting sustainable urbanization. J. Clean. Prod. **109**, 25–38 (2015)
8. Cabeza, R., Luis, J., Sanchez, C.S., Fuentes, G.F.J.: Past themes and tracking research trends in entrepreneurship: a Co-word, Cites and usage count analysis. Sustainability **11**, 3121 (2019)
9. Small, H., Griffith, B.C.: The structure of scientific literatures I: identifying and graphing specialties. Sci. Stud. **4**, 17–40 (1974)
10. Cambrosio, A., Limoges, C., Courtial, J.P., Laville, F.: Historical scientometrics? Mapping over 70 years of biological safety research with co-word analysis. Scientometrics **27**, 119–143 (1993)
11. Ying, D., Chowdhury, G.G., Foo, S.: Bibliometric cartography of information retrieval research by using co-word analysis. Inform. Process. Manag. **37**, 817–842 (2001)
12. Zong, Q., Shen, H., Yuan, Q., Hu, X., Hou, Z., Deng, S.: Doctoral dissertations of Library and Information Science in China: a co-word analysis. Scientometrics **94**, 781–799 (2013)
13. Diego, C.G. Marta, O.U.C. Eva-María, M.V.: Knowledge areas, themes and future research on open data: a co-word analysis. Gov. Inform. Q. **36**, 77–87 (2019)
14. Zhang, Q., Ma, F.C.: On paradigm of research knowledge management: a bibliometric analysis. J. Manag. Sci. China **10**, 65–74 (2007)
15. An, X.Y., Wu, Q.Q.: Co-word analysis of the trends in stem cells field based on subject heading weighting. Scientometrics **88**, 133–144 (2011)
16. Cho, C.H., Patten, D.M.: The role of environmental disclosures as tools of legitimacy: a research note. Account. Org. Soc. **32**, 639–647 (2007)
17. Tang, Y.H., Wu, S.M., Miao, X., Pollard, S.J.T., Hrudey, S.E.: Resilience to evolving drinking water contamination risks: a human error prevention perspective. J. Clean. Prod. **57**, 228–237 (2013)
18. Boston-Fleischhauer, C.: Enhancing healthcare process design with human factors engineering and reliability science, part 2: applying the knowledge to clinical documentation systems. J. Nurs. Adm. **38**, 84–89 (2018)
19. Davis, M.V., Macdonald, P.D.M., Cline, J.S., Baker, E.L.: Evaluation of public health response to hurricanes finds north carolina better prepared for public health emergencies. Public Health Rep. **122**, 17–26 (2007)
20. Gao, W.Y., Zhang, H., Luo, Y.: Preventing false negative results in detecting new coronavirus nucleic acid. Int. J. Lab. Med. **41**, 641–643 (2020)

Analytics for Big Data of Images and Test

An Analysis Model of Automobile Running State Based on Neural Network

Jie Yan[1], Xinxin Guan[2], Qingtao Zeng[1(✉)], Chufeng Zhou[3], Yeli Li[1], and Fucheng You[1]

[1] Beijing Institute of Graphic Communication, Beijing, China
zengqingtao@bigc.edu.cn
[2] National Museum of China, Beijing, China
[3] China Women's News, Beijing, China

Abstract. A reasonable design of the operating condition curve of automobile running state is conducive to improving the credibility of the government, so it is more and more important to formulate a test condition that reflects the actual road driving conditions in China. The actual fuel consumption is very different from the regulatory certification results. In order to construct the model mainly by two-segment clustering, the initial clustering of the processed data is carried out by self-organizing mapping neural network, and the cluster number and clustering center are obtained to solve the problem of poor convergence in the K-means model in the early stage. In view of the construction of the operating condition curve of the driving characteristics of light vehicles in a city, the data pre-processing, the extraction of motion fragments and the construction of the driving conditions of a car are to be provided for the driving data set of the same vehicle in a city.

Keywords: Automobile running state · Self-organizing mapping neural networks · K-means model · Two-segment clustering

1 Introduction

1.1 Background

In the early years, because China's development in the automotive industry is still relatively backward, so in the domestic automotive products for energy consumption or emission certification, choose to use the European NEDC (New European Drivig Cycle) driving conditions to complete the car certification, such a practice for China's automotive energy conservation and emission reduction and technology development has provided a lot of impetus to promote the development of China's automotive industry.

Subsequently, China's economic development is more and more rapid, the national economy continues to grow, China's car security also began to rise, gradually our country has been using NEDC driving conditions began to do not conform to China's national conditions, the use of NEDC conditions as the benchmark to optimize the calibration of the car, the actual situation and NEDC operating conditions of the data deviation is

Y. Weng et al. (Eds.): TridentCom 2020, LNICST 380, pp. 83–94, 2021.
https://doi.org/10.1007/978-3-030-77428-8_7

growing. Not only that, Europe and the United States in many years of development and practice also found that NEDC conditions of many shortcomings, in order to solve the problem, Europe and the United States began to implement the use of the world light vehicle test cycle. But even WLTC conditions are not realistic for our country. The two most important characteristics of this condition: idle time ratio and average speed, and China's actual car driving conditions there is a big difference. On the other hand, China's vast geographical area, the degree of development of each city, climatic conditions and traffic conditions are not the same, so that the characteristics of the car driving conditions in each city there are obvious differences. Mixed traffic consisting of non-motor vehicles such as motor vehicles and bicycles is the main feature of urban traffic in my country. According to statistics, non-motor vehicles, mainly bicycles, account for 25% to 55% of the total traffic. Because of their different driving behavior, speed and other basic characteristics, mixed traffic has a certain impact on urban road driving conditions. In my country's mixed traffic, motor vehicles and non-motor vehicles, fast vehicles and slow vehicles may run in the same lane and interfere with each other. Therefore, it is urgent to pass in-depth research, to develop in line with the actual road driving conditions of China's cars test conditions, as the automotive industry vehicle development and evaluation of the basis.

1.2 The Current State of Research at Home and Abroad

Domestic and foreign scholars have conducted a lot of research on how to construct local car driving conditions. The proposed construction methods mainly include short-stroke method, clustering method and Markov method. The short-stroke method uses short-stroke as the basic unit, and randomly combines all short-strokes. The random-combined short-stroke constitutes candidate operating conditions. The method of feature parameter evaluation is used for candidate operating conditions, and the candidate with feature parameters closest to the experimental data is selected. The conditions are representative driving conditions.

Foreign researchers have done a lot of research on driving conditions in some areas: KS Nesamani of the University of California and others established the driving conditions of urban buses in Chennai, India based on the data collected using GPS [1]; Nanyang, Singapore Sze-Hwee Ho and others at the Polytechnic University used the vehicle tracking method to construct vehicle driving conditions that are more in line with the actual road conditions in Singapore [2]; Matjaz Knez and others at the University of Mariol in Slovenia used the Tango GPS program to measure the importance of the actual driving of the vehicle. Parameters, and thus developed the driving conditions of the small town Celje in Slovenia [3]. There are also many achievements in the construction of actual driving conditions in China: Li Ning of Hebei Agricultural University and others used the short-stroke method to construct the road driving conditions of Tianjin through principal component analysis and cluster analysis [4]; Hefei University of Technology Qin, Ma Honglong and others used SOM network to cluster the principal components, and used the obtained weights as the initial clustering center of FCM clustering to construct the road driving conditions in Hefei [5]; Cai E, Li Yangyang of Chang'an University, etc. People constructed road driving conditions in Xi'an based on the K-means clustering algorithm [6].

2 Related Research

2.1 Self-organizing Map Neural Network

Model Overview. This modeling uses a neural network model, self-organizing map neural network (SOM), abbreviated as SOM. The SOM neural network model is mainly a method that can represent high-dimensional data in a low-dimensional space (usually one-dimensional or two-dimensional). The process of reducing the dimensionality of a vector is called vector quantisation. In addition, the SOM network can maintain the topological relationship of the original data. The self-organizing mapping neural network can map high-dimensional data to low-dimensional space through the neural network according to the characteristics of the sample and the internal rules, so as to achieve the purpose of dimensionality reduction and clustering. The structure diagram is shown in Fig. 1.

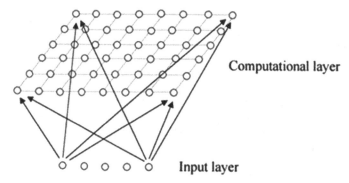

Fig. 1. SOM neural network structure diagram.

The link between the input layer and the output layer is primarily through the weight vector. The SOM neural network input layer corresponds to the input vector of the sample; Output Neuron nodes are widely connected to other nodes in the neighborhood, competing with each other for activation. At the same time only one neuron node is activated and the other neuron nodes are suppressed. This activated neuron node, called the winning unit, updates the weight of the winning unit and its adjacent regions, allowing the output node to maintain the topological characteristics of the input vector. However, the traditional SOM neural network still has some disadvantages, the number of neurons in the competitive layer needs to be pre-defined, the initial value of the right vector is randomly generated, this network structure restriction greatly affects the convergence speed and learning effect of the network.

2.2 Overview of the K-Means Model

The k-means clustering algorithm is a clustered analysis model of an iterative solution proposed by James MacQueen. The so-called clustering, that is, according to the principle of similarity, according to the degree of similarity divided into clusters, this is an unservesed process, the data object to be processed without any prior knowledge, prior knowledge is an indispensable part of the experience.

For the k-means model, there are two ways to terminate an iteration: one is to set the number of iterations T, and when the second iteration is reached, the iteration is terminated, at which point the resulting class cluster is the final clustering result [7].

The k-means model measures similarity between data objects, usually at Euclidean distance. Euclidean distance is calculated as follows:

$$dist(x_i, x_j) = \sqrt{\sum_{d=1}^{D} (x_{i,d} - x_{j,d})^2} \tag{1}$$

Where D represents the number of properties of the data object. $dist(x_i, x_j)$ represents Euclidean distance from x_i to x_j. $x_{i,d}$ represents the distance from xi to the nearest cluster center. $x_{j,d}$ represents the distance from x_j to the nearest cluster center.

k-means model in the process of clustering, the corresponding class cluster center because of continuous iteration re-update, corresponding to the class.

The average of all data objects in a cluster, that is, the center of the class cluster of the updated cluster. Defines the center of the class cluster for the kth class cluster is $Center_k$.

Updated as a formula (2).

$$Center_k = \frac{1}{|C_k|} \sum_{x_i \in C_k} x_i \tag{2}$$

Where C_k represents the kth class cluster; C_k represents the number of data objects in the kth class cluster. The leveling here refers to the level of all elements in class cluster C_k on each column property, so $Center_k$ is also a containing D.

Vector of properties, expressed as (3).

$$Center_k = (Center_{k,1}, Center_{k,2} \cdots Center_{k,D}) \tag{3}$$

For the k-means model, there are two ways to terminate an iteration: one is to set the number of iterations T when it comes to Up to the Tth iteration, the iteration is terminated, and the resulting class cluster is the final clustering result.

Square and criterion functions, function models such as formulas (4).

$$J = \sum_{k=1}^{K} \sum_{x_i \in C_k} dist(x_i, Center_k) \tag{4}$$

3   Improved Self-organizing Neural Mapping Network for Automotive Driving Conditions Construction

3.1   Basic Principle

The two-segment clustering model building K-means clustering model is a classic clustering model, but the model needs to give a exact number of clusters at the beginning, cluster center, otherwise it is easy to cause the model not convergence or local convergence problems. It was decided that the data set should be clustered before the K-means clustering model, and for this clustering, we chose to use the SOM self-organizing mapping neural network model to do so. The SOM model is an unsealed clustering method with good self-organization. During model operation, clustering is automatically based on the signs of the data, resulting in data that can be used for the number of clusters and cluster centers that the K-means model can enter. The resulting data is then used for the K-means model to solve the problem of pre-convergence of the K-means model.

3.2 Model Building

Here are the steps:

1. Mark the time break point in the data set and divide the data set into multiple segments according to the time break point.
2. Mark the acceleration and deceleration anomaly data in each segment, reject and further segment;
3. Long-term parking, long-term traffic jams, and long-term low-speed intermittent driving (maximum speed is less than 10 km/h) data to deal with;
4. Data that is often idled for more than 180 s is processed at a maximum value of 180 s;
5. After the above work is completed, according to the definition of the kinematic segments, the work of statistical kinematic segments is completed;
6. According to the data set after processing, a mathematical model is established, the characteristic data of the driving conditions of the car are calculated, and the driving conditions of the generation table are drawn.

3.3 Code Implementation

The algorithm pseudo-code is as follows Table 1.

Table 1. The model details the process description.

```
Input: Class cluster number K, iteration abort threshold δ.
Output: Clustered results.
For t=1,2,3…,T
    For every xᵢ
        Calculate dist(xᵢ,centerₖ) according to formula (1);
        Divide xi into the class clusters at the center of the closest class cluster;
    End for
    Update the center of all class clusters according to formula (5);
    According to formula (6), the interpolation Δ J of the two iterations is calculated;
    If Δ J<δ
        Then The result of the cluster is output;
        Break;
    End if
End for
```

4 Analysis of Experimental Results

4.1 The Experimental Process

First of all, on the data pre-processing, the first data cleaning. Wash away some dirty data to avoid affecting later results. Time is missing, acceleration and decrease speed are abnormal, and idle data is cleaned to ensure complete motion fragments. We select the vehicle from the parking idle zone of 0 to the parking idle interval of 0 for the next speed of 0 as a motion snippet. Calculate the average of the 15 indicator parameters selected in the motion fragment to form a feature parameter matrix. The initial cluster number K and cluster center Z are obtained by algorithm, and then the cluster number K and cluster center Z are used as inputs of K-means algorithm, and the cluster results are output. Finally, the driving conditions are constructed according to the established database.

Due to the different conditions in the course of car driving, the original acquisition data recorded directly by the vehicle driving data collection equipment often contains some bad data values. In these data, the bad data mainly include several types: due to high-rise buildings covered or tunneled, GPS signal loss, resulting in the data provided in the time is not continuous, car add, reduce speed abnormal data, long-term parking collected abnormal data, long-term traffic jams, intermittent low-speed driving conditions. Take the following steps to clean the data in response to the above.

- Time loss: For time-missing data, the car into multiple high-rise buildings, covered by high-rise buildings, or the car into the tunnel, will cause the loss of GPS positioning of the car, resulting in data loss, that is, data time is not continuous problems, therefore, the data set should be segmented from the time breakpoint to ensure complete travel fragments.
- Acceleration and deceleration anomalies: For acceleration and deceleration anomaly data, an ordinary car should typically have an acceleration time of more than 7 s from 0–100 km/h while driving, so some transient accelerations in the data set can be considered abnormal data. For deceleration anomaly data, the maximum deceleration of the emergency brake is usually 7.5–8 m/s^2, so data that is outside this range can also be considered abnormal.
- Idle speed: For long-term idle data, there is a long-term parking in the process of car driving, such as: parking does not stop, stop and stop, but the car's equipment is still running, as well as traffic jams for too long, intermittent low-speed driving situation. In this case, it's all handled at idle speed, but when a period of idle time exceeds 180 s, we treat it as an exception and calculate it at a maximum of 180 s.

4.2   Extraction of Motion Fragments

In the process of studying and constructing the driving condition curve of the automobile, constructing the motion fragment of the vehicle of this model is the most common method used to complete the study. In general, the definition of a motion fragment refers to the vehicle from the speed of 0 parking idle interval to the next stop idle interval, after the processed data set, based on the data set, according to the definition of python fragments divided into multiple psychological fragments, and statistics related data. The driving condition curve and automobile motion characteristics of the automobile by constructing the model should represent the corresponding characteristics of the collected data source (processed data), and the smaller the error between the two, the better, indicating that the representative of the vehicle driving conditions constructed is better [8]. Driving conditions refer to a period of vehicle speed change, and its main parameters such as average vehicle speed and idle driving time should be consistent or as close as possible to the actual traffic conditions in the area [9]. The driving condition is expressed as a speed-time curve. Automobile gear shifting, speed selection, acceleration and deceleration have a great influence on automobile fuel consumption [10]. Therefore, the driving condition of the vehicle on the road is expressed by some parameters that can reflect its motion characteristics, such as acceleration, deceleration, constant speed and idling speed [11]. The following picture is an example of the construction of the car condition under the complete time segment, such as Fig. 2, Fig. 3 and Fig. 4.

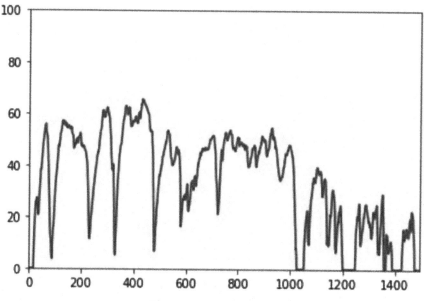

Fig. 2. Motion fragment 1

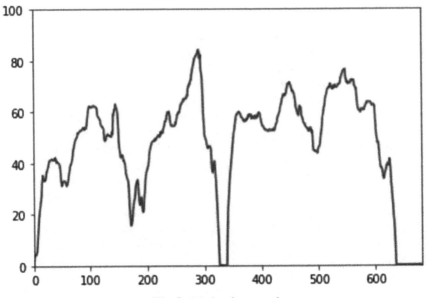

Fig. 3. Motion fragment 2.

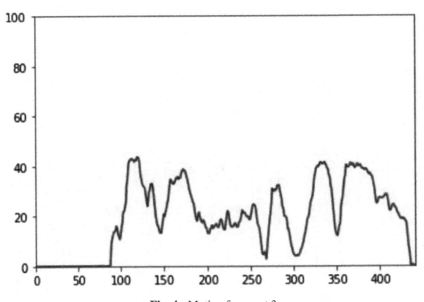

Fig. 4. Motion fragment 3.

4.3 Selection and Calculation of Feature Parameters

In order to construct the automobile motion characteristic evaluation system, 15 automobile motion characteristic evaluation indicators have been established. As shown in Table 2.

Table 2. Feature parameter indicator.

Serial number	Feature parameters	Meanings
1	$T(s)$	Running time
2	$S(m)$	Driving distance
3	$S_{ni}(m)$	Non-idle travel distance
4	$V(km/h)$	Average speed
5	$\bar{V}_{ni}(km/h)$	Average travel speed
6	$V_{max}(km/h)$	The maximum speed
7	$\bar{A}_a\left(m/s^2\right)$	Average acceleration
8	$\bar{A}_d\left(m/s^2\right)$	Average reduction
9	$F_i(\%)$	Idle time ratio
10	$F_a(\%)$	Acceleration time ratio
11	$F_d(\%)$	Deceleration time ratio
12	$V_s(km/h)$	The speed standard is poor
13	$V_{sa}(km/h)$	Increase the speed standard deviation
14	$V_{sd}(km/h)$	Reduce the speed standard deviation
15	$A_{sa}(m/s^2)$	Acceleration standard deviation

Here's our formula for calculating feature parameters.

$$S(m) = V_1T_1 + V_2T_2 + \cdots + VnTn \tag{5}$$

$$S_{ni}(m) = V_{1ni}T_{1ni} + V_{2ni}T_{2ni} + \cdots + V_{nni}T_{nni} \tag{6}$$

$$\bar{V}\left(\frac{km}{h}\right) = \frac{S}{T} \times 3.6 \tag{7}$$

$$\bar{V}_{ni}\left(\frac{km}{h}\right) = \frac{S - S_i}{T - T_i} \times 3.6 \tag{8}$$

$$\bar{A}_a\left(\frac{m}{s^2}\right) = \frac{\frac{\Delta V_{a1}}{\Delta t_1} + \frac{\Delta V_{a2}}{\Delta t_2} + \cdots + \frac{\Delta V_{an}}{\Delta t_n}}{n} \tag{9}$$

$$F_d(\%) = \frac{T_d}{T} \tag{10}$$

$$\bar{V}\left(\frac{km}{h}\right) = \frac{V_1 + V_2 + \cdots + V_n}{n} \tag{11}$$

$$V_s\left(\frac{km}{h}\right) = \sqrt{\frac{(V_1 - \bar{V})^2 + (V_2 - \bar{V})^2 + \cdots + (V_n - \bar{V})^2}{n}} \tag{12}$$

$$\bar{A}_{sa}\left(\frac{m}{s^2}\right) = \frac{A_{1sa} + A_{2sa} + \cdots + A_{nsa}}{n} \tag{13}$$

$$A_{sa}\left(\frac{m}{s^2}\right) = \sqrt{\frac{\left(A_{1sa} - \bar{A}_{sa}\right)^2 + \left(A_{2sa} - \bar{A}_{sa}\right)^2 + \cdots + \left(A_{nsa} - \bar{A}_{sa}\right)^2}{n}} \tag{14}$$

$$\bar{V}_a\left(\frac{km}{h}\right) = \frac{V_{1a} + V_{2a} + \cdots + V_{na}}{n} \tag{15}$$

$$V_{sa}\left(\frac{m}{s^2}\right) = \sqrt{\frac{\left(V_{1sa} - \bar{V}_a\right)^2 + \left(V_{2sa} - \bar{V}_a\right)^2 + \cdots + \left(V_{nsa} - \bar{V}_a\right)^2}{n}} \tag{16}$$

$$\bar{V}_d\left(\frac{km}{h}\right) = \frac{V_{1d} + V_{2d} + \cdots + V_{nd}}{n} \tag{17}$$

$$V_{sd}\left(\frac{m}{s^2}\right) = \sqrt{\frac{\left(V_{1sd} - \bar{V}_d\right)^2 + \left(V_{2sd} - \bar{V}_d\right)\bar{V}_d^2 + \cdots + \left(V_{nsd} - \bar{V}_d\right)^2}{n}} \tag{18}$$

4.4 Results and Analysis

The average of 15 indicator parameters is calculated, and the traditionally calculated driving conditions are constructed from the two-segment clustering method.

The operating conditions are compared with the driving conditions constructed separately using the k-means method, and the results are shown in Table 3.

Table 3. The results of the experiment were compared.

Feature parameters	Experimental data	K-means	Two-segment clustering
T(s)	14.49	14.49	14.49
S(m)	676.82	676.82	676.82
S_{ni}(m)	671.61	671.61	671.61
V(km/h)	14.52	14.01	14.63

(*continued*)

Table 3. (*continued*)

Feature parameters	Experimental data	K-means	Two-segment clustering
$\bar{V}_{ni}(km/h)$	21.81	20.83	22.34
$V_{max}(km/h)$	35.81	35.81	35.81
$\bar{A}_a\left(m/s^2\right)$	1.86	1.75	1.92
$\bar{A}_d\left(m/s^2\right)$	-2.11	-1.93	2.15
$F_i(\%)$	43.01	41.25	43.93
$F_a(\%)$	28.95	30.48	28.07
$F_d(\%)$	25.12	22.81	24.40
$V_s(km/h)$	11.8	11.8	11.8
$V_{sa}(km/h)$	1.59	1.72	1.51
$V_{sd}(km/h)$	1.76	1.59	1.81
$A_{sa}(m/s^2)$	2.59	2.57	2.57

The results show that the average relative error obtained by the two-segment clustering method is small, only 3%, and the error of K-means clustering method is greater than 5%. Therefore, the two-segment clustering method perfectly avoids the K-means clustering because the data set is too large, resulting in the initial convergence difficulties of the model run, there may be local optimal solution of the problem, and the model built by K-means represents the driving conditions closer to the experimental data to better reflect the actual road traffic conditions of the city in which the car is located.

5   Conclusion

Through the test, get a large number of actual driving speed data, experiment repeatability is better, through the obtained motion fragment analysis, the construction of driving conditions and Europe's NEDC and WLTC operating conditions are different, which proves that each city has different driving conditions characteristics, can not have some standard driving conditions to fully reflect.

Acknowledgments. 1. Major special project of science and technology of Guangdong Province, No: 190826175545233.

2. Beijing science and technology innovation service capability construction project (PXM2016_014223_000025).

3. BIGC Project(Ec202007).

References

1. Nesamani, K.S., Subramanian, K.P.: Development of a drivingcycle for intra-city buses in Chennai, India. Atmos. Environ. **45**(31), 5469–5476 (2011)

2. Ho, S.H., Wong, Y.D., Chang, W.C.: Developing Singapore Driving Cycle for passenger cars to estimate fuel consumption and vehicular emissions. Atmos. Environ. **97**, 353–362 (2014)

3. Knez, M., Muneer, T., Jereb, B., et al.: The estimation of a driving cycle for Celje and a comparison to other European cities. Sustain. Cities Soc. **11**(2–3), 56–60 (2014)

4. Li, N.: Construction and Research of Urban Road Vehicle Driving Conditions. Hebei Agricultural University, Baoding (2013)

5. Shiqin, M.H., Jianxun, D., et al.: Improved FCM clustering method and its application in the construction of driving conditions. China Mech. Eng. **25**(10), 1381–1387 (2014)

6. Wei, C., Li, Y., Li, C., et al.: Based on the K-average clustering algorithm, Xi'an automobile driving condition synthesis technology research. Autom. Technol. **8**, 33–36 (2015)

7. Jianping, G., Dexuan, R., Jianguo, X.: Construction of automobile driving conditions based on global K-means clustering algorithm. Henan Li J. Univ. Technol. (Nat. Sci. Edn.) **38**(01), 112–118 (2019)

8. Wang, Y., Zhang, N., Sun, Z., Wu, Y., Liu, B.: Vehicle driving condition recognition algorithm based on LVQ model. Agricul. Equip. Veh. Eng. **57**(05), 1 − 4+8 (2019)

9. Liu, X., Yan, D.: Investigation and research on driving conditions of urban vehicles in my Country. Environ. Sci. Res. **13**(1), 23–28 (2000)

10. Yang, Y., Cai, X., Du, Q., et al.: Research on driving conditions of road vehicles in Tianjin. Autom. Eng. **24**(3), 200–204 (2002)

11. Ma, Z., Zhu, X., Li, M., et al.: Dynamic clustering method in actual driving conditions of vehicles application in development. J. Wuhan Univ. Technol. **27**(11), 69–71 (2005)

Fusing BERT and BiLSTM Model to Extract the Weaponry Entity

Haojie Ge, Xindong You, Jialai Tian, and Xueqiang Lv[⊠]

Beijing Key Laboratory of Internet Culture Digital Dissemination, Beijing Information Science
and Technology University, Beijing, China
lxq@bistu.edu.cn

Abstract. Weaponry entity extraction is an indispensable link in the process of
constructing a weaponry knowledge graph. In terms of entity extraction of weapons
and equipment, a fusion model of domain BERT model and BILSTM model with
embedded word vectors and word conversion rate vectors is proposed to identify
weapons and equipment entities. First, the BERT model is used to perform pre-
training tasks on massive weaponry corpus. Secondly, the Word2vec model is
used to train the word vectors to provide a priori semantic information, and the
word conversion rate vector is embedded to input more a priori information to
the model. Finally, the hierarchical entity extractor extracts entities of different
categories. Experiments results show that the fusion model has strong coding
ability and sufficient prior knowledge, and the F1 value on the Global Military
Network corpus reaches 91.436%.

Keywords: Weaponry entity extraction · BERT · BILSTM · Word conversion
rate vector · Hierarchical entity extractor

1 Introduction

If the military builds a knowledge graph in the field of weapons and equipment, then they
will manage its weapons and equipment more efficiently. In other words, this knowledge
graph helps the military analyze its combat effectiveness, and obtain more information
on the weapons and equipment of competitors. There are a large number of unstruc-
tured texts containing weapon and equipment information on the Internet, which can
be extracted to form a weapon and equipment knowledge graph. Named entity recognition (NER) is an indispensable step in building a knowledge graph of weapons and
equipment.

Xiang Xiaowen [1] used the Hidden Markov model to carry out the Chinese named
entity recognition task. To fill the deficiencies of the model, its results were used with
rules to improve the recognition effect. The rules are as follows: selection rule, split rule,
supplementary call rule, boundary repair rule, consolidation rule. Feng Yuntian et al. [2]
used a conditional random field model to extract named entities from military texts, and
added feature templates and domain dictionaries to provide prior information to improve

© ICST Institute for Computer Sciences, Social Informatics and Telecommunications Engineering 2021
Published by Springer Nature Switzerland AG 2021. All Rights Reserved
Y. Weng et al. (Eds.): TridentCom 2020, LNICST 380, pp. 95–107, 2021.
https://doi.org/10.1007/978-3-030-77428-8_8

the extraction effect of military entities. In 2019, Li Jianlong [3] and others analyzed the difficulties of military text entity recognition and used a Bidirectional LSTM recurrent neural network model to solve the recognition problem of named entities in the military field. By adding a combination of word vectors and attention mechanisms. The LSTM recurrent neural network model is improved the recognition effect Ju Jiupeng et al. [4] used the method of combining conditional random fields and rules to identify the geographical space named entities in the text, using the BIO tagging scheme, adding part of speech, linguistic features, and text features to the feature template of the conditional random field, and adding hierarchical rules, company name rules, place name rules to improve the extraction effect. Zhang Hainan [5] used a deep neural network to perform named entity recognition tasks on the People's Daily corpus. To solve the problem of word segmentation tool segmentation errors and sentence length differences after segmentation affecting the network effect, the word hybrid embedded matrix was added to improve the extraction effect.

With the development of neural networks, the LSTM neural network model is widely used. Its ability to remember or forget text information determines its competence for natural language processing tasks. More and more scholars begin to use the LSTM neural network model to solve the problem of named entity recognition. Mourad Gridach [6] used the combination of LSTM neural network and conditional random field to recognize biological named entities, and the precision value is up to 90.27%. Ji Xiangbing [7] and others used the Attention-BILSTM method. The Attention mechanism can not only solve the long-distance dependence problem of traditional neural networks, but also increase the model's attention to special words, and give greater attention to important words to improve the effectiveness of the model. The language model has advanced the NLP tasks greatly. Google proposed the BERT [8] pre-training language model in 2018. BERT can be fine-tuned to adapt to various NLP tasks. Google has proved the effectiveness of BERT in various NLP tasks. BERT greatly improves the task of named entity recognition. Wang Ziniu [9] used BERT for the task of named entity recognition. It input the output vector of BERT into the LSTM-CRF layer to further extract the features and achieved an F1 value of 94.86% on its corpus.

The corpus of this paper is based on military texts. Military texts have their domain specificities. Because the texts are from the Internet, some irregular or networked names will increase the difficulty of recognition. At present, named entity recognition in the general field has received extensive attention and widely research, and has had practical effects, but few scholars researched named entity recognition in the military field. This paper collects a large number of military texts on the Internet, uses the BERT language model for pre-training based on this, and merges it with the BILSTM model with embedded word vectors and word conversion rate vectors, and finally uses a hierarchical entity extractor to extract entities to solve military text naming entity recognition problem.

2   Design of Weapon Equipment Entity Extraction Model

Figure 1 is a weapon and equipment entity recognition framework based on the fusion of BERT and BILSTM.

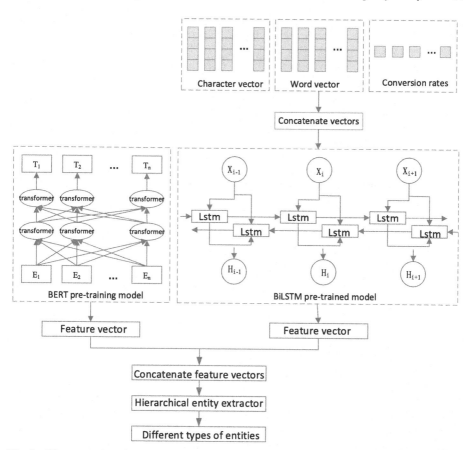

Fig. 1. Weapon and equipment entity recognition framework based on the fusion of BERT and BILSTM

This framework is based on the fusion of the BERT model and the BILSTM model to solve the problem of named entity recognition in weapon equipment. First, we pre-train the BERT language model on large-scale military texts and generate feature vectors after encoding the text through the pre-training BERT language model. Second, we use the Word2vec language model to train the word vector matrix, calculate the word conversion rate in the text to form a word conversion rate vector matrix, convert the text into a vector through the word vector matrix and the word conversion rate vector matrix, and input the vector into the BILSTM model to obtain the feature vector. Finally, the feature vectors output by the BILSTM model and the BERT language model are added to obtain the total feature vector, and the hierarchical entity extractor is used to extract the total feature vector to obtain different types of entities.

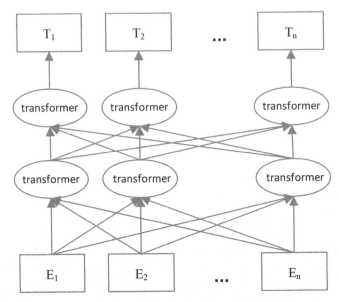

Fig. 2. Structure diagram of BERT model

2.1 BERT Pre-trained Language Model

The method of the BERT model adopts self-supervised learning which refers to supervised learning on the corpus without manual annotation. Using the BERT model to do pre-training tasks on a large number of military texts can encode the texts into vectors with military semantics, increase prior information and improve the model's ability to recognize weapons and equipment entities. Google has proved that the BERT model can transfer learning when the pre-training is completed, and it only needs to fine-tune the model input and output and model parameters when performing other NLP tasks.

The internal structure of BERT is shown in Fig. 2. The sentence gets E_1 to E_N vectors through word vector embedding and position embedding, and the final feature vectors T_1 to T_N are obtained through the transformer layer. The transformer includes an encoding structure and a decoding structure. It was originally used for machine translation tasks. However, it is applied to many NLP models at present because of its powerful feature extraction capabilities. In BERT, only the encoding structure of the transformer is used, but its decoding structure is discarded in that when the encoding structure is implemented, the current word can view the information of the front and rear words, while the current word of the decoding structure can only view the information of the previous word. Obviously, in the entity extraction task requires a coding structure that can obtain bidirectional information for which the BERT model is adapted. The reason for the Transformer's strong feature extraction ability is its internal Multi-Head Attention mechanism. Multi-Head Attention contains Self Attention mechanisms which are shown in Fig. 3. The specific operations of the Self Attention mechanism are as follows: the first step is the H vector passes through three different fully connected layers to obtain three vectors Q, K, and V. Then the second step is to obtain the vector Q

$\times$ K_T after matrix multiplication of Q and K_T, which represents the degree of correlation between words and other words.

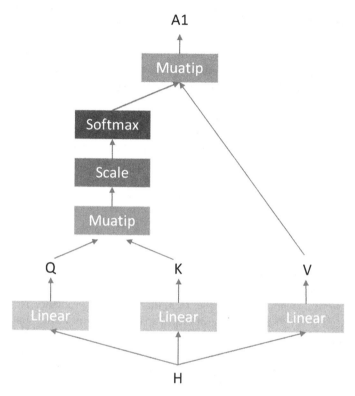

Fig. 3. Structure diagram of Self-Attention mechanism

The last step is to obtain the correlation degree vector between words by putting standardized Q $\times$ KT into the Softmax activation function, and then the correlation degree vector should be multiplied by V to obtain the vector A1. That is to say, each word in the BERT model will take into account the semantic weight of other words in the sentence when encoding, so it has a strong coding ability.

The pre-training of the BERT model includes two tasks. One is the task of predicting randomly masked words. Assuming that E_1 to E_N are known prior sentences, mask 15% of the words and let the model predict the masked words. The other task is to predict whether the next sentence belongs to the same article task as the current sentence. Supposed E_1 to E_{10} are the current sentence, and E_{10} to E_N are the next sentence, then the model try to predict whether E_1 to E_{10} and E_{10} to E_N belong to the same article. Experiments have proved that using the BERT model for pre-training tasks on military corpus can encode sentences into vectors that are closer to their real semantic information, thereby improving the effect of entity extraction.

2.2 BILSTM Input Vector Representation

At present, the neural network-based named entity recognition method misses many prior features in the text, such as word features. If we use word segmentation tools or domain vocabulary to segment the text to obtain phrases, then the length of the phrase after the segmentation will be smaller than the length after the word segmentation.

To ensure that the dimension of the vector obtained after the word embedding of the sentence is consistent, the word vector is copied to form a new copy of the word length. The word vector matrix and word vector matrix are trained by the Word2vec model. The shape of the word vector matrix is (N, 128), and N represents the number of words or the number of words, 128 is the predetermined vector dimension. After tagging the text, each word has a chance to be transformed into any label, and the transition probability of each word into each label can be calculated. The greater the transition probability, the greater the expected value of the corresponding label. By calculating the conversion probability of each word corresponding to the label, the conversion rate vector matrix is obtained. The calculation formula of transition probability is as follows:

$$p_{label}^{word} = \frac{Count_{label}^{word}}{Count_{word}} \tag{1}$$

p_{label}^{word} is the probability that a word is transformed into a specific label, which is equal to the total number of times the word is converted to the label divided by the total number of times the word appears. For example, in military texts, the sentence is: the aircraft carrier Liaoning is my country's first aircraft carrier, the entity in the sentence is the aircraft carrier Liaoning, and the name of the aircraft carrier category entity generally ends with the word ship. Assuming that the conversion rate of $p_1^{舰}$ship is calculated to be 0.98, the probability that the word ship is converted into a 1 tag is 0.98, which means that the probability of the word ship as the tail text of the named entity is 0.98. The number of rows of the conversion rate vector matrix is the number of words N, the number of columns is the number of tags NUMtag, and the matrix shape is (N, NUMtag). The text is transformed into the input vector of the BILSTM model in the shape of (Lenseq, 256 + NUMtag) through the word vector matrix and the word conversion rate vector matrix. Lenseq represents the length of the sentence.

2.3 Fusion of BILSTM and BERT Models

The BILSTM model can capture the bidirectional information flow of the text, and it has been proved to be suitable for named entity recognition tasks. In this paper, the text vector is input into the BILSTM model to obtain the feature vector. The BILSTM model structure is shown in Fig. 4, from Xi − 1 to Xi + 1 are inputs vector. The input vectors are input into the model from the forward direction and the reverse direction respectively to obtain the feature vectors from Hi − 1 to Hi + 1.

The learning results of different neural network models have certain differences. For example, when the BERT model judges that the label of the ship character is 1, the probability is 0.98, while the BILSTM model judges that the probability of the ship character's label is 1 is 0.45. The label probability should be half of the sum of the

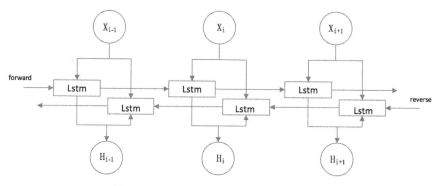

Fig. 4. Structure diagram of BILSTM model

probability results of the two models (0.715), and the predicted label of the ship character after the fusion of the two models should be 1, so the BERT model can correct the wrong results of the BILSTM model, and the BILSTM model can also correct the BERT model result. The feature vector of the BERT and the feature vector of BILSTM are added to obtain the feature vector with deeper semantic information of the text, which helps the hierarchical entity extractor to accurately extract the named entity.

Hierarchical Entity Extractor
When traditional neural networks use only one fully connected layer for sequence labeling, so only one label sequence can be generated per sentence. There are often multiple types of named entities in a sentence, and different types of named entities may overlap entities. For example, when the sentence is: The aircraft carrier Liaoning is China's first aircraft carrier, the target entity that needs to be extracted is the aircraft carrier Liaoning and Liaoning place named entities. Multiple fully connected layers are used to generate different types of labeling sequences to solve the overlapping problem of different types of named entities, which can also enhance the recognition ability of certain types of entities.

There are two types of labels in this paper: 0 and 1. A sentence will generate two-line tag sequences, one sequence is responsible for extracting the beginning text of the named entity, and the other sequence is responsible for extracting the ending text of the named entity. The sigmoid activation function is used to convert the output corresponding to each text into a value from 0 to 1. The size of the value indicates the degree to which the text is converted into a start text or an end text. When the corresponding value of the text is greater than 0.5, the text is taken as the start text or the end text.

The tag sequence generated by a sentence is shown in Fig. 5. The text extracted in sequence 1 is the beginning text of the entity, and the text extracted in sequence 2 is the ending text of the entity. The values 0.98 corresponding to the text in sequence 1 is greater than 0.5, so the text is extracted Liao is the beginning text of the entity, and the value 0.999 corresponding to the text ship in Sequence 2 is greater than 0.5, so the text ship is taken as the ending text of the entity. The final named entity extracted is the aircraft carrier Liaoning.

sequence2	0.98	0.0082	0.021	0.0298	0.09	0.052	0.0001	0.0008	0.0097	0.0056	0.0045
sequence1	0.01	0.001	0.08	0.076	0.12	0.034	0.999	0.0032	0.045	0.056	0.0954
sentence	辽	宁	号	航	空	母	舰	是	中	国	的

Fig. 5. Label sequence

3   Experiments

3.1   Dataset

The experimental data comes from the text data on ships and aircraft on the Global Military Network website, and finally, 5,000 sentences are marked. Among them, 4000 pieces are used as training data, 500 pieces are used as test data, and 500 pieces are used as verification data. The named entities of weapons and equipment in this article mainly consists of the following six categories: ships (the Nimitz aircraft carrier), aircraft (Black Hawk fighter), radar (Patriot radar), missiles (Sea Sparrow missile), systems (Aegis system), naval gun (11 m naval gun). An example of data labeled is shown in Fig. 6. The number 1 indicates that it is the beginning text of the weapon entity, and the letter after the "−" character is the English abbreviation of the entity category. For example, "jc" represents the ship category. The number 2 indicates that it is the ending text of the weapon entity, and "dd" indicates that the entity category is the missile category. The corresponding English abbreviations of entity categories are shown in Table 1, and the number of weapon and equipment entity categories in the corpus is shown in Table 2, where each weapon entity category accounts for an even proportion.

辽/1-jc	宁/0	号/0	航/0	空/0	母/0	舰/0	是/0	我/0	国/0
第/0	一/0	艘/0	航/0	空/0	母/0	舰/0	，/0	其/0	上/0
搭/0	载/0	爱/1-dd	国/0	者/0	导/0	弹/2-dd	节/0	省/0	燃/0

Fig. 6. Examples of the data tags

3.2   Evaluation Index

To verify the effectiveness of the model, the F1 value after the combination of precision P and recall rate R is used to judge the pros and cons of the model. The calculation

Table 1. English abbreviation for the different categories

Entity category	Entity category abbreviation
Ship	jc
Aircraft	fj
Missile	dd
Naval gun	jp
Radar	ld
System	xt

Table 2. Corresponding quantity of weapon entity category

Entity category	Quantity
Ship	3645
Aircraft	3412
Missile	2800
Naval gun	2588
Radar	2136
System	2689

formulas are shown in Eqs. (2), (3), and (4). When the names and categories of the predicted entity and the real entity are the same, it is called the total number of correctly identified entities.

$$P = \frac{\text{Total number of correctly identified entities}}{\text{Total number of entities identified}} \times 100\% \qquad (2)$$

$$R = \frac{\text{Total number of correctly identified entities}}{\text{Total number of entities in the test data}} \times 100\% \qquad (3)$$

$$F1 = \frac{2 \times P \times R}{P + R} \times 100\% \qquad (4)$$

3.3 Experiments and Results Analysis

The model runs on the Ubuntu 16.04 operating system of the Dell server with 64G of memory. The GPU is 8 T V100 graphics cards, each of which has 16G of graphics memory, and the coding language is python3.6. We use the Keras deep learning framework. Through experiments, it is found that different model parameters correspond to different entity recognition results. The optimal parameters are finally determined by tuning as shown in Table 3.

Table 3. Parameter settings of the model

Parameter name	Parameter value
BERT word vector dimension	768
BERT pre-training Batch-Size	16
Maximum text length	256
BERT hidden layer dimension	768
BILSTM model layers	2
BERT-Dropout value	0.9
Number of BERT pre-training iterations	500
BILSTM-Dropout value	0.9
BILSTM word vector dimensions	200

To verify the feature extraction ability and transfer learning ability of BERT, we set up experiment 1 and 2. To prove that adding a layered entity extractor can more accurately identify weapon entities, we set up experiment 2 and 3. In all experiments, except for experiment 2, the layered entity extractor is not used, and other experimental models all use layered entity extractor. To verify that the BERT model pre-trained on the corpus of a specific domain is more suitable for named entity tasks than the pre-trained BERT model on the general domain corpus, we set up experiments 4 and 5. To verify the effectiveness of the BILSTM model combining embedded word vectors and conversion rate vectors, we set up experiment 3 and 5. The specific experiment content is as follows:

Experiment 1: uses the BILSTM model with embedded word vectors and word conversion rate vectors to perform named entity recognition tasks on the data set, and the name of the experiment is denoted as BILSTM-T.

Experiment 2: uses the BERT model that is pre-trained on the military text and has no hierarchical entity extractor to perform named entity recognition tasks on the data set. The experiment name is recorded as PRE-BERT-no hierarchical.

Experiment 3: uses the BERT model pre-trained on military texts to perform named entity recognition tasks on the data set, and the experiment name is recorded as PRE-BERT.

Experiment 4: uses Google's open-source Chinese pre-trained BERT model and the BILSTM model with embedded word vectors and word conversion rate vectors to fuse them on the data set to perform named entity recognition tasks. The experiment name is recorded as BERT-BILSTM-T.

Experiment 5: The BERT model pre-trained on military texts and the BILSTM model with embedded word vectors and word conversion rate vectors were used to fuse them on the data set for named entity recognition tasks. The name of the experiment is recorded as PRE-BERT-BILSTM-T.

The overall results of the five groups of experiments are shown in Fig. 7 and Table 4.

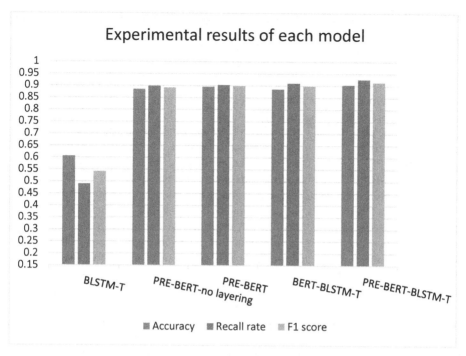

Fig. 7. Experimental results of each model

Table 4. Overall experimental results of the different models

Experiment no	Model name	Accuracy	Recall	F1 score
1	BILSTM-T	60.56	48.94	54.13
2	PRE-BERT-no layering	88.48	89.76	89.115
3	PRE-BERT	89.53	90.24	89.884
4	BERT-BILSTM-T	88.53	91.05	89.772
5	PRE-BERT-BiLSTM-T	90.32	92.58	91.436

To verify the powerful feature extraction and transfer learning capabilities of the BERT model, a comparison between experiment 1 (BILSTM-T) and experiment 2 (PRE-BERT-no layering) is carried out. The experimental results show that the F1 value of the BILSTM-T model that uses only the embedded word vector and the word conversion rate vector is increased by 35 percentage points using the BERT pre-training model, indicating that BERT has strong transfer learning capabilities and feature extraction capabilities. Only with self-supervised learning on the unlabeled corpus of the domain and fine-tuning the model for supervised learning on a small amount of labeled text, the model can achieve good results.

To prove that the addition of a layered entity extractor can more accurately identify weapon entities, this paper conducted a comparative experiment between Experiment 2 (PRE-BERT-no layering) and Experiment 3 (PRE-BERT). Experiment 3 (PRE-BERT) a layered entity extractor is added based on experiment 2 (PRE-BERT-no layering). The accuracy and recall rate of the model with a layered entity extractor is slightly higher than that of the model without a layered entity extractor, indicating that adding a layered entity extractor can extract a certain type of entity more accurately.

To verify the effectiveness of the BILSTM model fused with embedded word vectors and conversion rate vectors, this paper conducted a comparative experiment of Experiment 3 (PRE-BERT) and Experiment 5 (PRE-BERT-BILSTM-T), Experiment 5 (PRE-BERT)-BILSTM-T) based on Experiment 3 (PRE-BERT), a BILSTM model that combines embedded word vectors and conversion rate vectors. Experiment 5 (PRE-BERT-BILSTM-T) compared with experiment 3 (PRE-BERT), the accuracy rate and recall rate increased by 0.79% and 2.34%, respectively. The recall rate increased significantly which shows that adding embedded word vectors and conversion rate vectors not only allows the model to acquire more prior features, but model fusion can correct the recognition errors of a single model, thereby improving the effectiveness of named entity recognition.

To verify the effectiveness of the pre-trained BERT model for specific domain corpus, this paper conducts a comparative experiment of experiment 4 (BERT-BILSTM-T) and experiment 5 (PRE-BERT-BILSTM-T) which based on Experiment 4 (BERT-BILSTM-T): the general domain corpus is changed to the military corpus. The accuracy and recall rate of the BERT model pre-trained with military corpus are both about 2% higher than that of the BERT pre-training model in the general field. It indicates that the pre-training BERT model on the military corpus can learn the prior features of the military corpus and thus increase the effect of named entity recognition in the military field.

Therefore, the BERT model pre-trained on the military text and the BILSTM model (PRE-BERT-BILSTM-T) with embedded word vectors and word conversion rate vectors are more suitable for the task of weapon equipment named entity recognition.

4   Conclusion

BERT model is used to conduct self-supervised training on the military corpus to obtain the military corpus pre-training BERT model and integrates the BILSTM model embedded with word vectors and word conversion rate vectors to solve the problem of weapon equipment named entity recognition. Experimental results show that the BERT model has strong transfer learning capabilities and feature extraction capabilities. The pre-trained BERT model on the specific domain corpus can encode sentences into vectors that are closer to their real semantic information, thereby increasing the effect of a domain named entities. Adding a layered entity extractor can extract a certain type of entity more accurately. The embedded word vector and word conversion rate vector can increase the prior features of the domain, and the model fusion makes the models correct each other. The model in this paper is effective for the task of weapon equipment named entity recognition.

Acknowledgments. This work is supported by National Natural Science Foundation of China under Grants No. 61671070. Project of Developing University Intension for Improving the Level of Scientific Research–No. 2019KYNH226, Qin Xin Talents Cultivation Program, Beijing Information Science & Technology University No. QXTCP B201908.

References

1. Xiang, X., Shi, X., Zeng, H.: A Chinese named entity recognition system combining statistics and rules. Comput. Appl. **25**(10), 2404–2406 (2005)
2. Feng, Y., Zhang, H., Hao, W.: Named entity recognition for military texts. Comput. Sci. **42**(7), 15–18, 47 (2015)
3. Li, J., Wang, P., Han, Q.: Military named entity recognition based on two-way LSTM. Comput. Eng. Sci. **4**, 20 (2019)
4. Ju, J., Zhang, M., Ning, J., et al.: Geospatial named entity recognition combining CRF and rules. Comput. Eng. **37**(7), 210–212 (2011)
5. Zhang, H., Wu, D., Liu, Y., et al.: Chinese named entity recognition based on deep neural network. Chinese J. Inform. **31**(4), 28–35 (2017)
6. LNCS Homepage. http://www.springer.com/lncs. Accessed on 21 Nov 2016
7. Ji, X., Zhu, Y., Li, F., et al.: Chinese named entity recognition based on Attention-BiLSTM. J. Hunan Univ. Technol. **5**, 14 (2019)
8. Devlin, J., Chang, M.W., Lee, K., et al: BERT: Pre-training of deep bidirectional transformers for language understanding (2018). arXiv:1810.04805
9. Wang, Z., Jiang, M., Gao, J., et al.: Chinese named entity recognition method based on BERT. Comput. Sci. **46**(11A), 138–142 (2019)

CIC Chinese Image Captioning Based on Image Label Information

Xindong You[1], Likun Lu[2(✉)], Hang Zhou[1], and Xueqiang Lv[1]

[1] Beijing Key Laboratory of Internet Culture and Digital Dissemination Research, Beijing Information Science and Technology University, Beijing, China
{youxindong,lxq}@bistu.edu.cn
[2] Beijing Institute of Graphic Communication, Beijing, China
lklu@bigc.edu.cn

Abstract. Although image captioning technology has made great progress in recent years, the quality of Chinese image description is far from enough. In this paper, we focus on the problem of Chinese image captioning with the aim to improve the quality of Chinese image description. A novel framework for Chinese image captioning based on image label information (CIC) is proposed in this paper. Firstly, image label information is extracted by a multi-layer model with shortcut connections. Then the label information is input into the neural network with an extension of LSTM, which we coin L-LSTM for short, to generate the Chinese image descriptions. Extensive experiments are conducted on various image caption datasets such as Flickr8k-cn, Flickr30 k-cn. The experimental results verify the effectiveness of the proposed framework (CIC). It obtains 27.1% and 21.2% BLEU4 average values of Flickr8k-cn and Flickr30k-cn, respectively, which outperforms the state-of-art model in Chinese image captioning domain.

Keywords: Chinese image caption · Convolution neural network · Recurrent neural network · Deep learning · Chinese image tagging

1 Introduction

Image caption is an important work in the field of computer vision and natural language processing. It can generate descriptive sentences according to the image content, which is an effective method to narrow the "semantic gap" [1] between low-level visual feature and semantic information of the image [2–4]. Image caption is useful and practical for many application scenarios, including helping children or impaired people understand images, visual intelligent chat robot and image retrieval, which has great commercial value and attracted the great interest of researchers [5, 6]. However, image caption is a challenging task, which not only needs to recognize the objects in the image, but also needs to use the natural language to represent the attributes of objects, and then organized the relationship between them by natural language manner.

Up to now, there are three kinds of methods to generate image captions, they are template-based methods, retrieval-based methods, and deep learning-based methods,

Y. Weng et al. (Eds.): TridentCom 2020, LNICST 380, pp. 108–119, 2021.
https://doi.org/10.1007/978-3-030-77428-8_9

among which the deep learning-based methods are most advanced and achieve the best performance. Deep learning models, usually use the "encoder-decoder" framework. An image is encoded as a vector using a convolution neural network (CNN) and captions are decoded from the vector using a recurrent neural network (RNN) for end-to-end training of the entire system [13–17]. Currently, much of the image captioning work is concentrating on generating English sentences. Few image captioning work conducted on Chinese sentence generated due to the lack of datasets on image description labeled by Chinese. Rich meanings of Chinese words and the complex sentence structure make the Chinese image description be more challenging work. In this paper, we focus on Chinese image caption issues. We propose a label-based image caption model (CIC). Firstly, we design an image label prediction network with higher accuracy for image label feature generation. Secondly, the L-LSTM proposed in this paper which uses the image label features obtained from the label prediction network to generate descriptive sentences. Finally, we optimize the loss function by using label features, which further improves the quality of descriptive sentences. Extensive experiments conducted on various benchmark datasets such as Flickr8k-cn, Flickr30k-cn show that CIC achieves state-of-the-art performance.

The rest of this article is arranged as follows. We review the related work about image caption in Sect. 2, then introduce the proposed model CIC in Sect. 3, and show the experimental results in Sect. 4, finally give the conclusion in Section.

2 Related Work

Traditional image captioning methods can be divided into two categories: template-based methods and retrieval-based methods.

Template-based methods first use an object detector to detect the objects in the image, predict the object attributes and the relationship between objects, then fill the pre-designed template and finally form descriptive sentences [7–9]. Template-based methods are heavily dependent on the quality of object detection and limited by the pre-designed template, the generated descriptive sentences are single and lack of diversity. Retrieval-based methods first retrieve a similar subset of the images to be described in the training set based on the image visual feature, then generate candidate descriptive sentences by reasonably organizing the corresponding descriptive sentences of the similar subset images, and finally sort the candidate descriptions and select the optimal results [10–12]. The retrieval-based methods rely excessively on the training dataset, and the resulting descriptions are limited to the descriptions of the training set. With the rise of deep learning, these two kinds of methods are no longer favored.

With the development of deep learning, researchers have proposed image captioning methods based on deep learning. In 2015, Vinyals et al. proposed the image captioning model (Neural Image Caption, NIC) based on convolution neural network and Long Short-Term Memory (LSTM) [13]. The NIC model uses CNN to extract the visual feature of the image and takes the feature as the input of LSTM. The LSTM outputs the predicted words in turn to describe the contents of the image. The model is relatively simple, but the quality of generated sentences needs to be improved. Subsequently, the researchers improved on the NIC model. In 2015, Xu et al. introduced the Attention

Mechanism (AM) into the model for the first time, which enables the model to capture the local information of the image [14]. In 2016, Jia et al. used semantic information to guide LSTM in generating descriptions [15]. In 2017, Rennie et al. applied reinforcement learning to model training of image caption [16]. The objective of the existing model training is to maximize the probability of generating the correct descriptive sentence, which is inconsistent with the evaluation criteria in the inference. The method based on reinforcement learning can directly optimize the evaluation index in training, and obtain better results. In 2017, Dai et al. optimized the NIC model using Conditional GAN, making the generated sentences more natural and diverse [17]. In 2018, Anderson et al. proposed a combined bottom-up and top-down attribute mechanism [18], which enables the model to obtain image regions with significant semantics when predicting descriptions, and the performance is further improved.

The above-related work is all about the research on English image caption, the research on Chinese image caption is relatively few, and the quality of descriptions is needed to be improved. In 2017, Ze-Yu Liu et al. fused visual features and label features with LSTM in four ways to improve the effectiveness of the NIC model [19]. In 2018, Wei-Yu Lan et al. used the top10 image prediction labels to sort and select the generated sentences of NIC model, which makes the selected sentences closer to the label information and improves the image descriptive ability of NIC model [20].

3   CIC: Label-Based Chinese Image Captioning Model

We first describe the image label prediction network FC-PT in Sect. 3.1, then introduce our proposed image caption generator CIC in Sect. 3.2, the training process of the model is explained finally.

3.1   Image Label Prediction Network FC-PT

In the dataset of image caption, each picture described by five descriptive sentences, each sentence can vividly describe the content of the image. We choose the nouns, verbs, and adjectives in the sentence as the image labels. More specifically, Firstly, we use Chinese word segmentation tool Boson to segment the words in the descriptive sentences and selectively retain the nouns, verbs, and adjectives according to the word frequency. Then we construct a label vocabulary of the remaining words and tag the label information for each picture, therefore we can obtain the training data of label prediction network. Figure 1 shows the part-of-speech distribution of Flickr8k-cn and Flickr30k-cn dataset image labels.

The image label prediction network proposed in this paper consists of two parts, one is a feature extraction network based on CNN, the other is a feature classification network. as shown in Fig. 2

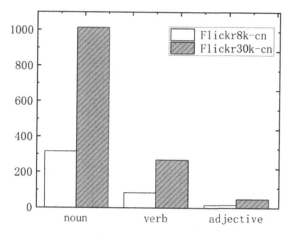

Fig. 1. Part-of-speech distribution of Flickr8k-cn and Flickr30k-cn

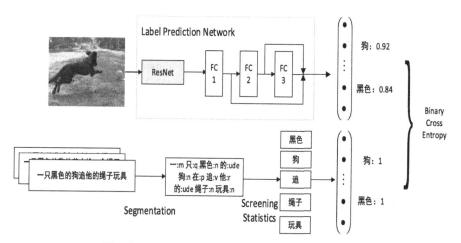

Fig. 2. Image label prediction classification network

3.2 CIC: Label-Based Chinese Image Captioning Model

The Chinese image captioning model CIC proposed in this paper is composed of CNN and L-LSTM. CNN is used as the encoder to extract image convolution features, and L-LSTM is used as the decoder to decode the image convolution features to the target descriptive sentences. Specifically, L-LSTM first accepts the image convolution feature and ignores the output at this time. Then, after inputting a start symbol <Start> and a predicted label feature, L-LSTM outputs a vector composed of the predicted probability of the words in the vocabulary and selects the word with the highest probability as the output. Then the word and the prediction label feature are used as the input of the next time, and the prediction is continued until the end symbol <End> is predicted, and the overall structure is shown in Fig. 3.

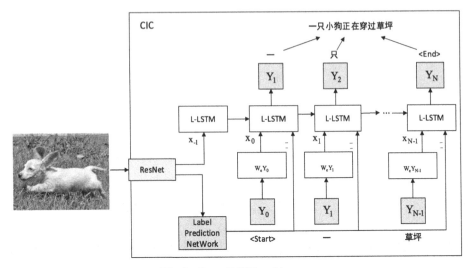

Fig. 3. Overall CIC architecture

The encoder CNN in the CIC model is a neural network used to process grid data. CNN model consists of a series of linear or non-linear transformation modules such as convolution layer, pooling layer, and activation layer. Deep CNN model is generally used to extract image features. After multiple times of convolution, pooling and activation of image data, the extracted features are more abstract and more expressive, which make breakthroughs in image classification, object detection, and other visual tasks. The CNN used in this model is ResNet-152. ResNet-152 is the best performance of ImageNet 2015 Image Classification Competition.

4 Experiment

4.1 Datasets

The datasets used in this paper are Flickr8k-cn and Flickr30k-cn. Flickr8k-cn and Flickr30-cn have been translated from English image caption datasets Flickr8k and Flickr30k into Chinese by machine translation method in Reference [21]. The Flickr8k-cn dataset contains 8,000 annotated images and 40,000 Chinese description sentences, as shown in Fig. 5. The Flickr30k-cn dataset contains 30,000 annotated images and 150,000 Chinese description sentences as shown in Fig. 6. In this paper, Flickr8k-cn and Flickr30k-cn are segmented according to the data segmentation method used in Kapathy et al. [22]. Flickr8k-cn includes 6000 training data, 1000 verification data, 1000 test data, Flickr30k-cn includes 28000 training data, 1000 verification data, 1000 test data (Fig. 4).

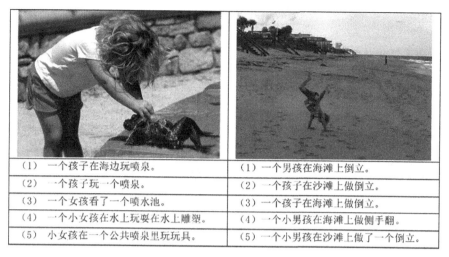

（1） 一个孩子在海边玩喷泉。	（1） 一个男孩在海滩上倒立。
（2） 一个孩子玩一个喷泉。	（2） 一个孩子在沙滩上做倒立。
（3） 一个女孩看了一个喷水池。	（3） 一个孩子在海滩上做倒立。
（4） 一个小女孩在水上玩耍在水上雕塑。	（4） 一个小男孩在海滩上做侧手翻。
（5） 小女孩在一个公共喷泉里玩玩具。	（5） 一个小男孩在沙滩上做了一个倒立。

Fig. 4. Examples of Flickr8k-cn dataset

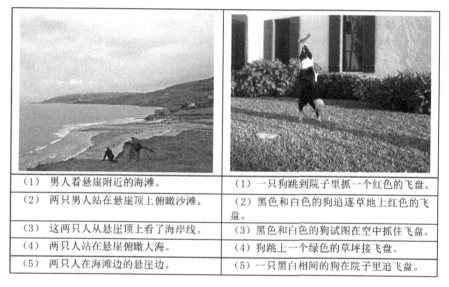

（1） 男人看悬崖附近的海滩。	（1） 一只狗跳到院子里抓一个红色的飞盘。
（2） 两只男人站在悬崖顶上俯瞰沙滩。	（2） 黑色和白色的狗追逐草地上红色的飞盘。
（3） 这两只人从悬崖顶上看了海岸线。	（3） 黑色和白色的狗试图在空中抓住飞盘。
（4） 两只人站在悬崖俯瞰大海。	（4） 狗跳上一个绿色的草坪接飞盘。
（5） 两只人在海滩边的悬崖边。	（5） 一只黑白相间的狗在院子里追飞盘。

Fig. 5. Examples of Flickr30k-cn dataset

4.2 Experiment Details

The lab environment is configured as follows: Intel Xeon E5-2603 v4 processor, 64G RAM, Nvidia Tesla k80 graphics card, operating system Ubuntu 16.03.1, development language python 2.7, and deep learning framework tensorflow 1.6.

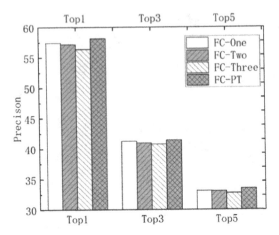

Fig. 6. Comparison of Flickr8k-cn accuracy

The Flickr8k-cn training set includes 6000 images, 30000 Chinese descriptive sentences, and 7784 words. The Flickr 30k-cn training set includes 28,000 images, 140,000 Chinese descriptive sentences, and 19735 words. In order to eliminate the interference of low-frequency words, we empirically preserve the nouns, verbs, and adjectives that appear at least twice in the five Chinese descriptive sentences of the same picture in Ref. [20], and the words whose overall word frequency is more than 20 times are used as the label vocabulary. Finally, the Flickr8k-cn label vocabulary contains 416 words, and the Flickr30k-cn label vocabulary contains 1330 words.

Label prediction network parameter configurations, as shown in Table 1.

Table 1. Label prediction network configuration parameters

Parameter name	Flickr8k-cn	Flickr30k-cn
Batch size	256	256
Learning rate	0.001	0.001
Number of epochs	50	50
ResNet-152 image feature dimension	2048	2048
Number of hidden layer units	512	1024
Dropout	0.5	0.5

The Chinese Image Captioning Model CIC parameter configurations, as shown in Table 2.

Table 2. The Chinese image captioning model CIC configuration parameters

Parameter name	Flickr8k-cn	Flickr30k-cn
Batch size	100	100
Learning rate	0.001	0.001
Number of epochs	50	50
Number of L-LSTM units	512	512
ResNet-152 image feature dimension	2048	2048
Word embedding dimension	512	512
Label feature dimension	416	1330
Loss optimization coefficient α	0.2	0.2

4.3   Evaluating the Proposed Label Prediction Network

Tables 3, 4, and 5 show the results of micro_Precision@k, micro_Recall@k, and micro_F1@k for different label prediction networks. FC-One represents the single-layer fully connected network. FC-Two represents the two-layer fully connected network. FC-Three represents the three-layer fully connected network. FC-PT represents our proposed label prediction network. We take Flickr8k-cn label prediction network results in Table 5 as an example to compare the proposed FC-PT network with FC-One, FC-Two, FC-Three. Experiments show that with the increase of network depth, network degradation occurs, that is, the accuracy and recall rate of the net decrease. The accuracy between FC-One and FC-Three decreases by 0.5% and the recall rate decreases by 0.57%. The FC-PT proposed in this paper is based on FC-Three network with residual structure, which improves the accuracy and recall rate to 33.49% and 39.54%, respectively. It shows that the proposed method can solve the problem of multi-layer label prediction network degradation. But as a whole, the accuracy and recall rate of label prediction network still have much room for improvement, which needs to be further studied in the future.

Table 3. Label prediction network top1 results comparison

Network structure	Flickr8k-cn			Flickr30k-cn		
	micro_Precision@1	micro_Recall@1	micro_F1@1	micro_Precision@1	micro_Recall@1	micro_F1@1
FC-One	57.43%	13.56%	21.94%	46.10%	8.44%	14.27%
FC-Two	57.17%	13.50%	21.84%	45.73%	8.37%	14.15%
FC-Three	56.40%	13.32%	21.55%	44.89%	8.22%	13.89%
FC-PT	58.16%	13.73%	22.22%	46.39%	8.49%	13.36%

Table 4. Label prediction network top3 results comparison

Network structure	Flickr8k-cn			Flickr30k-cn		
	micro_Precision@3	micro_Recall@3	micro_F1@3	micro_Precision@3	micro_Recall@3	micro_F1@3
FC-One	41.29%	29.25%	34.24%	35.39%	19.43%	25.09%
FC-Two	40.99%	29.04%	34.00%	34.65%	19.03%	24.57%
FC-Three	40.78%	28.89%	33.82%	34.60%	19.00%	24.53%
FC-PT	41.47%	29.38%	34.39%	35.45%	19.47%	25.13%

Table 5. Label prediction network top5 results comparison

Network structure	Flickr8k-cn			Flickr30k-cn		
	micro_Precision@5	micro_Recall@5	micro_F1@5	micro_Precision@5	micro_Recall@5	micro_F1@5
FC-One	33.12%	39.11%	35.87%	29.92%	27.39%	28.60%
FC-Two	33.08%	39.06%	35.82%	29.56%	27.06%	28.25%
FC-Three	32.72%	38.63%	35.43%	29.01%	26.56%	27.73%
FC-PT	33.49%	39.54%	36.26%	30.34%	27.77%	29.00%

Figure 7 specifically illustrate that portion of the Precision in the table. As shown in Fig. 7, the prediction accuracy of the network decreases with the increase of network depth, and the network FC-PT proposed in this paper adds a residual structure on the basis of FC-Three, which improves the prediction accuracy and verifies the effectiveness of the method proposed in this paper.

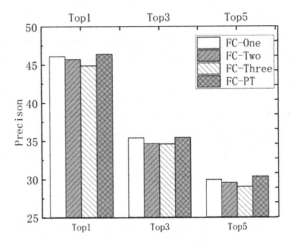

Fig. 7. Comparison of Flickr30k-cn accuracy

4.4   Evaluating the Proposed Chinese Image Captioning Model (CIC)

The proposed Chinese image caption network CIC is compared with CNIC-Ensemble in Ref. [17] and sentence rearrangement-MLP in Ref. [18]. As shown in Table 6, BLEU4, ROUGE-L, and CIDEr are greatly improved. Compared with CNIC-Ensemble, the experimental results are improved by 5.9%%, 2.1%, and 22.6%, and compared with sentence rearrangement-MLP, the experimental results are improved by 1.7%, 1.7%, and 2.4%. First, the improvement of Bleu indicates that the generated sentence has more co-occurrence words with the reference sentence, and the description is more accurate. Second, the improvement of ROUGE-L indicates that the generated description has higher accuracy and recall rate. Again, a significant increase in the CIDEr indicates that the generated sentence is more similar to the reference sentence. As shown in Table 7, CIC also performs well on Flcikr30k data. The CIC proposed in this paper has achieved the best results on Flickr8k-cn and Flickr30k-cn due to the existing Chinese image captioning model.

Table 6. Comparison of Flickr8k-cn Chinese image caption networks

Method	BLEU4	ROUGE-L	CIDEr
NIC19	18.7	44.2	27.9
CNIC-Ensemble 19	20.5	45.4	30.1
Google Model 20	23.6	44.8	47.4
Word rearrangement-MLP 20	23.4	44.9	47.2
Sentence rearrangement-MLP 20	24.7	45.8	50.3
CIC	26.4	47.5	52.7

Table 7. Comparison of Flickr30k-cn Chinese image caption networks

Method	BLEU4	ROUGE-L	CIDEr
NIC19	–	–	–
CNIC-Ensemble 19	–	–	–
Google Model 20	18.2	40.0	32.5
Word rearrangement-MLP 20	18.0	39.9	32.5
Sentence rearrangement-MLP 20	20.0	41.9	35.6
CIC	19.9	42.0	38.1

5 Conclusion and Future Work

We propose a label-based image captioning model CIC in this paper. Firstly, a label prediction network is proposed to capture the image label features, which effectively solves the problem of network degradation with the deepening of the number of label prediction network layers. Secondly, we present an L-LSTM architecture, in which image label features are input into the image caption network. However, the model proposed in this paper still has room for improvements. In the aspect of label prediction network, it will continue to improve the accuracy of label prediction network and try to use high-quality label features to generate descriptive sentences. In image caption network, more network architectures can be constructed, such as introducing image local features through the attention mechanism to further improve all aspects of the generation network indicators.

Acknowledgments. This work is supported by National Natural Science Foundation of China under Grants No. 61671070, Defense-related Science and Technology Key Lab Fund project 61420061903011, National Language Committee of China under Grants ZDI135-53, and Project of Developing University Intension for Improving the Level of Scientific Research–No. 2019KYNH226, Qin Xin Talents Cultivation Program, Beijing Information Science & Technology University No. QXTCP B201908.

References

1. Cui, P., Zhu, W., Chua, T.S., et al.: Social-sensed multimedia computing. IEEE Multimedia **23**(1), 92–96 (2016)
2. Li, X., Uricchio, T., Ballan, L., et al.: Socializing the semantic gap: a comparative survey on image tag assignment, refinement, and retrieval. ACM Comput. Surv. **49**(1), 14:1–14:39 (2016)
3. Ariji, Y., Yanashita, Y., Kutsuna, S., et al.: Automatic detection and classification of radiolucent lesions in the mandible on panoramic radiographs using a deep learning object detection technique. Oral Surg. Oral Med. Oral Pathol. Oral Radiol. **128**(4), 424–430 (2019)
4. Zhuge, Y., Zeng, Y., Lu, H.: Deep embedding features for salient object detection. In: Proceedings of the AAAI Conference on Artificial Intelligence, vol. 33, pp. 9340–9347 (2019)
5. Agrawal, A., Lu, J., Antol, S., et al.: VQA: visual question answering. Int. J. Comput. Vis. **123**(1), 4–31 (2015)
6. Das, A., Kottur, S., Gupta, K., et al.: Visual dialog. In: IEEE Conference on Computer Vision & Pattern Recognition. IEEE Computer Society (2017)
7. Farhadi, A., Hejrati, M., Sadeghi,, M.A., et al.: Every Picture Tells a Story: Generating Sentences from Images. Computer Vision – ECCV 2010, pp. 15–29. Springer, Berlin (2010)
8. Yang, Y., Teo, C.L., Hal Daumé, III., et al.: Corpus-guided sentence generation of natural images. In: Conference on Empirical Methods in Natural Language Processing. Association for Computational Linguistics (2011)
9. Kulkarni, G., Premraj, V., Ordonez, V., et al.: Babytalk: understanding and generating simple image descriptions. IEEE Trans. Pattern Anal. Mach. Intell. **35**(12), 2891–2903 (2013)
10. Kuznetsova, P., Ordonez, V., Berg, A.C., et al.: Collective generation of natural image descriptions. In: Proceedings of the 50th Annual Meeting of the Association for Computational Linguistics: Long Papers, vol. 1. Association for Computational Linguistics (2012)

11. Verma, Y., Gupta, A., Mannem, P., et al.: Generating Image Descriptions Using Semantic Similarities in the Output Space (2013)
12. Ordonez, V., Kulkarni, G., Berg, T.L.: Im2Text: describing images using 1 million captioned photographs. In: International Conference on Neural Information Processing Systems, pp. 1143–1151. Curran Associates Inc. (2011)
13. Vinyals, O., Toshev, A., Bengio, S., et al.: Show and tell: a neural image caption generator. In: IEEE Conference on Computer Vision and Pattern Recognition, pp. 3156–3164. IEEE Computer Society (2015)
14. Xu, K., Ba, J., Kiros, R., et al.: Show, attend and tell: neural image caption generation with visual attention. In: Proceedings of the 32nd International Conference on Machine Learning, pp. 2048–2057. JMLR. org, Lille (2015)
15. Jia, X., Gavves, E., Fernando, B., et al.: Guiding the long-short term memory model for image caption generation. In: IEEE International Conference on Computer Vision, pp. 2407–2415. IEEE (2016)
16. Rennie, S., Marcheret, E., Mroueh, Y., Ross, J., Goel, V.: Self-critical sequence training for image captioning. In: Proceedings of the IEEE Conference on Computer Vision and Pattern Recognition, pp. 7008–7024. Hawaii (2017)
17. Dai, B., Fidler, S., Urtasun, R., et al.: Towards Diverse and Natural Image Descriptions via a Conditional GAN (2017). arXiv:1703.06029
18. Anderson, P., et al.: Bottom-up and top-down attention for image captioning and visual question answering (2018). arXiv:1707.07998
19. Liu, Z.Y., Ma, L.L., Wu, J., Sun, L.: Chinese image captioning method based on multimodal neural network. J. Chin. Inform. Process. 31(06), 162–171 (2017)
20. Lan, W.Y., Wang, X.X., Yang, G., Li, X.R.: Improving chinese image captioning by tag prediction. Chin. J. Comput. 1–14 (2018)
21. Li, X., Lan, W., Dong, J., et al.: Adding Chinese captions to images. In: Proceedings of the 2016 ACM on International Conference on Multimedia Retrieval, pp. 271–275. ACM, New York (2016)
22. Karpathy, A., Li, F.F.: Deep visual-semantic alignments for generating image descriptions. Computer Vision and Pattern Recognition, pp. 3128–3137. IEEE (2015)

Cross-language Transfering the Patent Quality Evaluation Model Based on Active Learning Data Extension

Jiaqi Liu, Xindong You, Zhe Wang, and Xueqiang Lv[✉]

Beijing Key Laboratory of Internet Culture Digital Dissemination, Beijing Information Science and Technology University, Beijing, China
lxq@bistu.edu.cn

Abstract. At present, China has become a major patent production country, and the number of patent applications has been ranked first in the world for many years. As the number of patents has increased, the quality of patents has begun to draw people's attention. At present, there is no clear evaluation method for Chinese patents. Manual evaluation of patents requires a large number of relevant experts to research and compare patents in different fields, which is time-consuming and labor-intensive. In the previous study, the author constructed an English patent quality evaluation model PQE-MT using U.S. Patents that represent patent strength. This paper introduces this model into Chinese patents through transfer learning and active learning, thereby reducing the workload of manual labeling. The evaluation results show that the method in the experiment has achieved a good migration effect, with Micro-F1 reaching 74%.

Keywords: Patent quality assessment · Transfer learning · Active learning · Multi-task learning · Cross-language text classification

1 Introduction

In recent years, Sino-US trade disputes and US sanctions against Huawei have all reflected the importance of technological innovation and intellectual property rights. Traditional manufacturing industries need rapid transformation, which also reflects the importance of invention patents. China's R&D spending rose from 0.9% of GDP in 2000 to 2.22% in 2018. The total investment is nearly 2 trillion yuan [1]. It can be seen that the country has made great efforts to develop technology and actively innovate. In recent years, the number of entity patent applications in China has increased rapidly. In 2018, the number of patents applied by Chinese applicants was 1.542 million, up 11.6% year on year [2]. Under the phenomenon that the number of patent applications is leading the world, it does not mean that China's technological innovation is already at the top of the world. There are still some quality problems in China's patents, such as low application rate and lack of patents with important strategic significance and substantial improvement. It can be seen that China still lags behind other developed countries in terms of

Y. Weng et al. (Eds.): TridentCom 2020, LNICST 380, pp. 120–133, 2021.
https://doi.org/10.1007/978-3-030-77428-8_10

innovation, and the increase in the number of patent applications masks the fact that the quality of patents is low.

Based on these problems, putting high-quality patents in a strategic position has become an urgent task. Improving the quality of Chinese patents is of great significance to China's development. For enterprises, it is helpful to help enterprises understand the development trend of industry technology and choose the development direction in a targeted way [3]. From the perspective of the government, it is conducive to the government agencies to efficiently analyze the trend of science and technology, optimize the investment in science and technology, and formulate targeted policies for the development of science and technology. At the same time, it is helpful for scientific research institutions to analyze scientific and technological trends, grasp scientific and technological trends, track scientific and technological hot spots, and clarify technological directions [4]. Besides, the improvement of China's patent quality helps investors and patent inventors to analyze the direction of emerging technologies, quickly find better investment and development goals, and reduce potential legal risks.

Using data mining and natural language processing technologies, effective indicators are extracted from a large number of patent information data of different dimensions, and the US patent quality evaluation model PQE-MT is constructed. On this basis, using transfer learning and active learning methods, the index distribution and writing differences of Chinese patents have been improved.

2 Related Work

Due to the time-consuming and labor-intensive work of data labeling and the scarcity of high-quality labeling data, transfer learning has attracted more and more attention from the academic community. Banea [5] proposed a method of cross-language transfer learning due to the abundant data of English tagging. In this paper, the tagged corpus of English data is used to generate the source domain data set of the target language through machine translation, which proves the feasibility of using machine translation for cross-language transfer learning. Pan [6] proposed to transfer the domain with sufficient training data to the domain with similar data distribution, to greatly improve the learning effect by avoiding expensive data labeling work through knowledge transfer, and discussed the relationship between transfer learning and related machine learning technologies such as domain adaptation and sample selection deviation. Xu [7] uses migration learning and multitask learning to extract and transfer useful knowledge from the data in the auxiliary domain, thus helping to solve the problem of insufficient data in the target domain. The latest progress in the field of biological information is introduced. Weiss [8] explains transfer learning and information about solutions and discusses possible future research work. Where the migration learning solution is independent of data size. Yosinski [9] studied the mobility of deep neural networks. Fine-tune experiments are carried out layer by layer on different layers to explore the mobility of the network. It is pointed out that adding fine-tune to the deep migration network will greatly improve the effectiveness and better overcome the differences between data. The migration of network layers can accelerate the learning and optimization of the network. The bottom network learns the common characteristics and the top network learns the domain characteristics.

Transfer learning still needs to label a small amount of corpus for the model to adapt to the distribution of data features in the target domain. Active learning can predict the results through the model and select the samples that contribute the most to the improvement of the model. Tohompson [10] uses the method of active learning to try to select the example with the largest amount of information as the training data for transfer learning. The experimental results show that active learning can significantly reduce the number of labeled samples when the algorithm achieves the same effect. Tong [11] uses pool-based active learning. The algorithm does not need a randomly selected training set and can mark the requested samples. A new algorithm for active learning using a support vector machine provides a theoretical basis for the algorithm by using the concept of version space. The experimental results show that the active learning method in this paper can significantly reduce the demand for labeled samples. Settles [12] introduces active learning and reviews relevant literatures. Machine learning algorithms can achieve higher accuracy through fewer labeling training examples. The query scheme is discussed, and the experience and theoretical evidence of active learning are analyzed. Li Jielong [13] takes the minimum classification distance of SVM as the confidence level of selecting examples and proposes multi-example multi-label active learning based on the minimum classification interval of SVM, which effectively reduces the amount of sample labeling and improves the classification performance. Zhou [14] uses active learning and transfer learning, data expansion, majority selection, continuous fine-tuning, and other methods to verify the data set in the field of medical images, and points out that the introduction of active learning can reduce the amount of data annotation by at least half. Zhu [15] combines GAN with active learning for the first time, obtains the generator model by training GAN, and obtains the most valuable samples through active learning for experts to the label. Konyushkova [16] solves the problem of the insufficient generalization ability of traditional selection strategies. By transforming active learning into regression problems for learning, the experimental results have achieved good results on data sets in many different fields.

3   Cross-language Transfering Patent Quality Evaluation Model Based on Active Learning Data Extension

3.1   Prediction Model of Chinese Patent Quality Grade

Based on the PQE-MT model, this paper uses transfer learning and active learning methods to further propose a cross-language transfer patent quality evaluation model based on active learning data expansion, and transfer the original model to Chinese patents. The following article will introduce the model from these two parts respectively.

3.2   PQE-MT Model Structure and Transfer Learning

The PQE-MT model consists of two parts: a quantitative index model and a multi-task learning model. Multi-task learning includes text classification tasks and named entity recognition tasks. The following describes the specific content and functions of each part of the network model. The overall model structure is shown in Fig. 1.

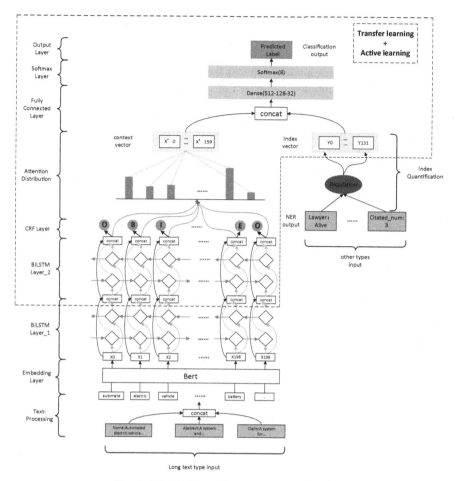

Fig. 1. PQE-MT model structure and migration

- Input: Initial Patent Attribute + Patent Title, Abstract, Claims.
- Index quantification: 132 indexes, composed of 15 initial indexes and 117 multidimensional quantified indexes.
- Text processing: The patent title, abstract, and sovereign claim are spliced together, and stop words and special symbols are removed. Convert all characters to lowercase letters and roots for English text; Word segmentation is carried out for Chinese texts.
- Word embedding: BERT [17] is used as the embedding layer of the model in the experiment. BERT is a pre-training model, which trains the language model on 3.3 billion text corpus and makes fine adjustments on different downstream tasks. The model has achieved the best results so far on different text tasks. BERT is a combination of Transformer. Transformer has made model innovations in multi-head attention mechanism, self-attention mechanism, and position coding. BERT enhances the semantic expression of sentences by learning contextual relationships in the large-scale corpus.

In the experiment, the word vector fine-tuned by BERT on the corpus in the field of new energy vehicles is used as the embedding of words.

- Bidirectional LSTM: After the embedding layer, the experiment uses multitask learning as part of the sequence model. Multitask learning includes two tasks: bi-directional LSTM, text classification task composed of attention mechanism, CRF, and named entity recognition task. The long-term memory network [18] can learn the long-term dependency of texts. The structure uses storage units to record historical information, thus ensuring the integrity of the information. The concept of the control gate is introduced, and the information flow of the model is controlled by the update gate, forgetting gate, and output gate. Based on LSTM, bidirectional LSTM takes into account the past and future timing features of the sequence, and effectively uses context information to mine more hidden features.
- Attention mechanism: When the input sequence is very long, LSTM is difficult to obtain a reasonable vector. Note that the machine retains the intermediate vectors of the LSTM encoder, and then trains a structure to selectively learn these inputs and associate the output sequence with them so that the model can focus on some words considered important in the input sequence.
- CRF: In the Named Entity Recognition task, the results of the bidirectional LSTM are entered into the CRF. CRF improves the accuracy of identification through the dependency relationship between tags. The words in the sentence correspond to each time node in the sequence. The output of the model is a series of tags, and the tag space is defined as {B, I, E, O}. "B" denotes the beginning of the domain term, "I" denotes the middle part of the domain term, "E" denotes the end of the domain term, and "O" denotes that the element does not belong to the domain term. According to the tag sequence output by the model, the domain words in the sequence can be determined.
- Fully connected layer: input a fully connected neural network composed of 512, 128, and 32 nodes.
- SoftMax Layer: The structure of the full connection layer is finally input into SoftMax Layer for multi-classification.
- Output: Eight types of patent quality grades.

The experiment uses US patents as the source domain and Chinese patents as the target domain. Due to the problem of language barrier between different languages, it is impossible to directly transfer between different languages. This involves the problem of cross-language text classification. At present, the mainstream solutions include methods based on language knowledge base [19], methods based on multilingual models [20] and methods based on machine translation technology [21]. The main research contents of this paper are as follows: 1. It is difficult to build a complete and accurate language knowledge base, which needs to be updated for different fields; 2. The effect of the existing machine translation has been greatly improved, and the experiment itself does not need very accurate translation, only the translation of domain words needs to be as accurate as possible; 3. The difference of feature space between different languages can help the model learn different features. In the experiment, machine translation was used to translate the text parts of Chinese and English patents, and the patent grades of some Chinese patents were marked. Through transfer learning, the model was adapted to the index distribution and language features of Chinese patents [22].

Through comparative experiments, the parameters of different layers are frozen to obtain the best offset effect. The specific experimental process and results will be explained in detail in the experimental results and analysis in the fourth part. Finally, the part shown by the dotted line in Fig. 1 is selected for the migration of model parameters.

3.3 Efficient Transfer Using Active Learning

Figure 2 is the flow chart of active learning.

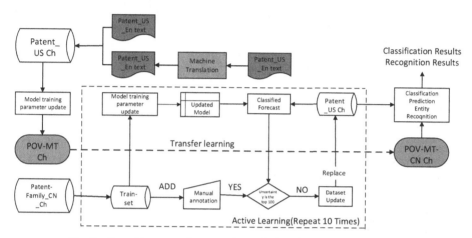

Fig. 2. Overall process diagram of transfer learning and active learning

4 Experimental Results and Analysis

4.1 Experimental Data

The experiment used 59,147 U.S. Patents, of which the number of patents with different ratings is shown in Fig. 3. 90% of the samples (53475) are selected as training data and 10% of the samples (5942) are selected as test sets for testing. The verification method selects the K-fold cross-validation for model optimization. K-1/K of the training data is selected as the training set and the rest as the verification set. As a result, the average value of K times is obtained, and the value of K is set to 10.

There are 21,611 Chinese patents, 308 of which exist in the U.S. Patent data set, i.e. 308 patents are applied in two countries at the same time, forming a patent family and belonging to the same family. In the experiment, its score in the US patent corresponds to the Chinese patent, so as to obtain the quality level corresponding to the Chinese patent. In this paper, 100 Chinese patents with the patent rating are obtained as the test set of the final model, another 208 are used as the initial migration data, and the remaining 21303 unlabeled Chinese patents are used as the data pool for active learning to select the data to be labeled.

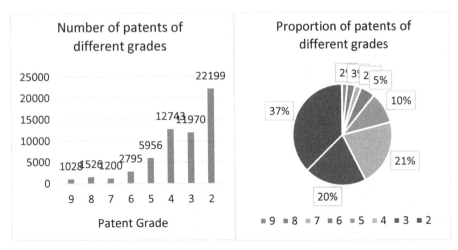

Fig. 3. Number and proportion of patents with different ratings

All the data in the experiment are randomly scrambled and the extraction method is random, to ensure the uniform distribution of different label samples and the accuracy and fairness of the experimental results. The machine translation part involved in this article uses Google Translation, which is currently the most accurate translation system.

4.2 Evaluation Indicators

The accuracy, recall, F-score, accuracy, Micro-averaging, and Macro-averaging used in text classification evaluation are used for evaluation. The calculation process is shown in formula (1)–(6). For Category C, the classification results can be divided into the following situations:

1) Originally Category C was divided into Category C, and the quantity was recorded as a;
2) Originally non-C was classified as C, and the quantity was recorded as B;
3) Originally Class C was classified as Non-C, and the quantity was recorded as C;
4) Originally non-C was classified as non-C, and the quantity was recorded as D;

$$Micro\_P = \frac{\sum_{i=1}^{n} a_i}{\sum_{i=1}^{n} a_i + \sum_{i=1}^{n} b_i} \tag{1}$$

$$Micro\_R = \frac{\sum_{i=1}^{n} a_i}{\sum_{i=1}^{n} a_i + \sum_{i=1}^{n} c_i} \tag{2}$$

$$Micro\_F1 = \frac{2 * Micro\_P * Micro\_R}{Micro\_P + Micro\_R} \tag{3}$$

$$Macro\_P = \frac{1}{n} \sum\nolimits_{i=1}^{n} P_i \tag{4}$$

$$Macro\_R = \frac{1}{n} \sum\nolimits_{i=1}^{n} R_i \tag{5}$$

$$Macro\_F1 = \frac{2 * Macro\_P * Macro\_R}{Macro\_P + Macro\_R} \tag{6}$$

4.3 Parameter Setting

The experiment uses a 768-dimensional BERT vector with 12-layer transformer and 12 multi-head attention mechanisms as the embedding layer of the model. When the accuracy rate of the verification set does not increase after 10 epoch, the training is stopped, and the best model parameters are obtained by the checkpoint. Besides, the experiment hopes to obtain a more accurate classification model in the multi-task learning of the experiment. The final loss value of the model is the sum of the loss value of the classification result and the loss value of the entity labeling result according to the weight of 3:1. Due to the imbalance of categories, the experiment gives corresponding class weight to different categories, so that the number of categories and the weight of each category are multiplied to the same value, ensuring that better results can be achieved in small categories. Based on this, the above models are compared and tested to obtain the best sequence model, which is combined with the quantitative index model. The active learning process is set up in 10 rounds. Each round obtains the top 100 data with the highest score for labeling, and finally obtains 1000 labeled samples for further migration training of the model.

4.4 Model Training Results

Selection of Transfer Layer in Transfer Learning.

The layers of the final PQE-MT are shown in Table 1:

For neural networks, different layers of the network model usually learn the characteristics of different levels of samples. "Visualizing and Understanding Convolutional Networks" [23] visualizes each layer of CNN, which shows the above theory more clearly. Layer1 and Layer2 learn basic color and edge features; Layer3 learns texture features; Layer4 learn local features such as wheel; Layer5 learns more discernible overall features. Compared with images, it is easier to observe, and the knowledge learned by each model of the text sequence is difficult to display, but in general it also conforms to the above-mentioned rules, and the bottom layer learns the features of part of speech and meaning of words. Learn semantic and syntactic features at a high level.

The experimental results list the micro-average and macro-average of accuracy, recall rate, and F value on the training set and the test set respectively. The results are shown in Table 2.

Table 1. PQE-MT layer information

Number of layers	Type	Output shape	Parameter quantity
0	Text Input Layer	(None, 200)	0
1	Embedding Layer	(None, 200,768)	17999616
2	Bidirectional LSTM_1	(None, 200, 160)	543360
3	Bidirectional LSTM_2	(None, 200, 160)	154240
4	Attention	(None, 160)	32400
5	Number Input Layer	(None, 132)	0
6	Concatenate Layer	(None, 292)	0
7/9/11	Dense Layer_1/2/3	(None, 512/128/32)	150016
8/10/12	Dropout Layer_1/2/3	(None, 512/128/32)	65664
13	CRF Layer	(None, 200, 4)	4128
14	Softmax Layer	(None, 8)	668

Table 2. Final results of different migration parts

Migration layer	Training set (micro avg/macro avg)						Test suite (micro avg/macro avg)					
	Precision		Recall		F1-score		Precision		Recall		F1-score	
0–14	0.85	0.70	0.85	0.68	0.85	0.69	0.61	0.38	0.60	0.44	0.60	0.41
2–14	0.83	0.70	0.83	0.63	0.83	0.66	0.66	0.43	0.65	0.46	0.65	0.44
3–14	0.82	0.66	0.82	0.65	0.82	0.65	0.66	0.61	0.66	0.54	0.66	0.57
7–14	0.78	0.66	0.77	0.60	0.77	0.63	0.60	0.44	0.60	0.38	0.60	0.41
9–14	0.60	0.43	0.60	0.39	0.60	0.41	0.58	0.44	0.58	0.36	0.58	0.40
11–14	0.53	0.37	0.53	0.34	0.53	0.35	0.52	0.42	0.52	0.35	0.52	0.38

We conducted a model migration experiment using only English texts of Chinese patents as training data and not using U.S. Patents, and compared with the 3–14 layer model with the best transfer effect to observe the improvement of model effect by transfer learning. The two results are shown in Tables 3 and 4.

Through the comparison of Tables 3 and 4, it can be seen that transfer learning has a certain degree of improvement on each index of the model. Due to the lack of training samples in normal supervised learning, the whole model has two obvious problems: first, the prediction results of the model are very poor in categories with a small number of samples, and the main measurement indexes, accuracy rate, recall rate and F value results in categories 7 and 8 are all 0; Second, the generalization ability of the model is very poor, and the over-fitting problem is obvious. Whether it is micro-average or macro-average, the test set is about 35% lower than the training set. Comparing the results after transfer learning, we can see that the results have improved on both issues.

Table 3. Result of training network use only Chinese patent data

Category	Training set				Test set			
	Precision	Recall	F1-score	Support	Precision	Recall	F1-score	Support
1	0.92	1.00	0.96	61	0.55	0.66	0.60	35
2	0.79	0.70	0.74	33	0.41	0.39	0.40	18
3	0.80	0.82	0.81	49	0.18	0.19	0.19	21
4	0.61	0.69	0.65	29	0.30	0.30	0.30	10
5	0.42	0.65	0.51	17	0.33	0.38	0.35	8
6	1.00	0.80	0.89	5	0.00	0.00	0.00	3
7	0.00	0.00	0.00	9	0.00	0.00	0.00	3
8	0.00	0.00	0.00	5	0.00	0.00	0.00	2
Micro avg	0.76	0.76	0.76	208	0.40	0.40	0.40	100
Macro avg	0.57	0.58	0.57	208	0.22	0.24	0.23	100

Table 4. Results of data transfer learning for initial 208 Chinese patent English text

Category	Training set				Test set			
	Precision	Recall	F1-score	Support	Precision	Recall	F1-score	Support
1	1.00	0.92	0.96	61	1.00	0.77	0.87	35
2	0.83	0.91	0.87	33	0.54	0.78	0.64	18
3	0.82	0.92	0.87	49	0.78	0.67	0.72	21
4	0.81	0.72	0.76	29	0.20	0.20	0.20	10
5	0.50	0.76	0.60	17	0.35	0.75	0.48	8
6	0.40	0.40	0.40	5	0.33	0.33	0.33	3
7	0.60	0.33	0.43	9	0.67	0.33	0.44	3
8	0.75	0.60	0.67	5	1.00	0.50	0.67	2
Micro avg	0.83	0.83	0.83	208	0.66	0.66	0.66	100
Macro avg	0.71	0.70	0.70	208	0.61	0.54	0.57	100

For categories with a small number of samples, the model has a better adaptation. For the prediction results, on the training set and the test set, the gap between the micro-average values is reduced to 17%, and the macro-average values are reduced to 10%, 16%, and 15% respectively. These two problems have been solved to a certain extent, thanks to the fact that the model has learned how relevant features affect the results in a large number of U.S. Patents. Although the distribution of features is somewhat different, the overall trend is roughly the same. In the process of transfer learning, the model further adapts to the changes of Chinese patents in various index items on the originally learned trend.

Although the model has been improved, the effect still cannot meet the final patent evaluation requirements. I hope to improve the effectiveness of the model by increasing the migration data.

In the experiment, 200 unlabeled Chinese patents were randomly selected for manual labeling as data_random, and the top 200 Chinese patents with the largest classification margin were labeled as data_active_learning by using an active learning algorithm. In the experiment, the two data sets are respectively incremented by 20 from 0 until reaching 200. The effects of random data selection and active learning data selection on model migration were compared. The comparison of the prediction accuracy of the model in the two cases is shown in Fig. 4.

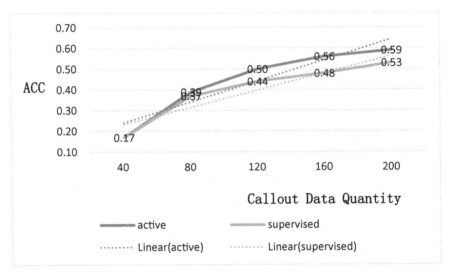

Fig. 4. Comparison of accuracy rate of active learning and randomly selected annotation data migration learning

Through the comparison of the two trend lines, it is found that the active learning selection data is better than the randomly selected data migration learning, and the model effect is equivalent to the random selection of 200 data annotation when the active learning selects about 140 data annotation. Therefore, the experiment uses active learning to further expand market data. Active learning can obtain data with the largest amount of information. In the experiment, 10 rounds of active learning were carried out, and the top 200 data with the largest classification margin were obtained for manual labeling in each round. A total of 2,000 labeled samples were obtained as new migration data, increasing the amount of data by only 10 times. The model uses the 2–14 layers with the best migration effect obtained by experimental comparison as the migration part, and the migration results of 2208 Chinese patent data obtained by active learning expansion are shown in Table 5. Besides, the experiment was carried out, in the same way, using the patented English language, and the results are shown in Table 6.

Table 5. Results of data transfer learning for 2208 Chinese patent english text after active learning expansion

Category	Training set				Test set			
	Precision	Recall	F1-score	Support	Precision	Recall	F1-score	Support
1	0.93	0.96	0.95	676	0.93	0.83	0.88	35
2	0.85	0.71	0.77	404	0.88	0.78	0.82	18
3	0.79	0.85	0.81	506	0.74	0.81	0.77	21
4	0.59	0.77	0.67	258	0.39	0.70	0.50	10
5	0.61	0.64	0.62	154	0.50	0.38	0.43	8
6	0.41	0.54	0.47	69	0.33	0.33	0.33	3
7	0.63	0.54	0.58	87	0.33	0.67	0.45	3
8	0.78	0.37	0.50	54	1.00	0.50	0.67	2
Micro avg	0.79	0.80	0.79	2208	0.74	0.74	0.74	100
Macro avg	0.70	0.67	0.68	2208	0.64	0.63	0.63	100

Table 6. Results of data migration learning for 2208 Chinese patents after active learning expansion

Category	Training set				Test set			
	Precision	Recall	F1-score	Support	Precision	Recall	F1-score	Support
1	0.95	0.89	0.92	676	0.87	0.79	0.83	35
2	0.68	0.68	0.68	404	0.51	0.54	0.53	18
3	0.65	0.79	0.71	506	0.52	0.64	0.57	21
4	0.55	0.52	0.53	258	0.45	0.42	0.43	10
5	0.45	0.28	0.34	154	0.36	0.22	0.27	8
6	0.43	0.36	0.39	69	0.33	0.67	0.45	3
7	0.56	0.71	0.48	87	0.33	0.33	0.33	3
8	0.70	0.65	0.67	54	1.00	0.50	0.67	2
Micro avg	0.73	0.71	0.72	2208	0.62	0.61	0.61	100
Macro avg	0.61	0.61	0.61	2208	0.55	0.51	0.53	100

The experimental results in Table 4 are compared with those in Table 5 to observe the influence of active learning and data expansion on the model effect. Using the model of initial data migration, the Micro-F1 values on the training set and the test set are 83% and 66%, and the Macro-F1 values are 70% and 57%, respectively. The overall model tends to over-fitting. After active learning for data expansion, Micro-F1 values are 79% and 74%, Macro-F1 values are 68% and 63%, respectively. Due to the increase in the amount of migrated data, the generalization ability of the model becomes stronger, and the effect of the model is improved to a certain extent when predicting the test set data.

The experimental results in Tables 5 and 6 are compared to observe the influence of Chinese and English languages on the model effect. It can be observed that the transfer effect of the model on English text is generally better than that on Chinese text. The author thinks that due to the limitation of machine translation technology when using the source model trained by US patent, the use of Chinese data after machine translation leads to the deterioration of the initial model effect and the reduction of the final transfer model effect. However, the overall influencing factors of English texts translated by Chinese patents, which are used in quantity and as target models, are relatively low. Besides, the differences in writing specifications and feature spaces between Chinese and English also make the learning effects of the models different.

5 Conclusions

By comparing and analyzing the patent data between China and the United States, the experiment summarizes the similarities and differences between the two countries' patents, aligns the quantitative indicators, and migrates to Chinese patents through the multi-task learning network PQE-MT model trained by the United States patent with patent quality rating labels. The transfer process mainly involves the selection of transfer parts, cross-language transfer, and the use of active learning to expand data. The advantage of this model lies in the use of migration learning technology and active learning to select the data to be labeled with the largest amount of information, thus minimizing the time-consuming manual labeling process. In the whole process, through experiments, the prediction effect of the model was gradually improved, and finally, the Chinese patent quality evaluation model achieved good accuracy. At the end of the experiment, the effect of transfer learning between Chinese and English was compared, and it was found that the result indicators were different, and the model learned different features. In the following work, the author will combine the two language models and consider the different features learned so that they can influence each other and improve the final results.

Acknowledgments. This work is supported by National Natural Science Foundation of China under Grants No. 61671070. Project of Developing University Intension for Improving the Level of Scientific Research–No. 2019KYNH226, Qin Xin Talents Cultivation Program, Beijing Information Science & Technology University No. QXTCP B201908.

References

1. In 2018. China spent nearly 2 trillion yuan on research and development, and major scientific and technological innovation indicators steadily improved. East China Sci. Technol. **2019**(04), 13 (2018)
2. China News Network. State Intellectual Property Office: In 2018, China filed 1.542 million invention patents [EB/OL]. (2019-1-10) [2019-6-21]. http://money.163.com/19/0110/16/E56 3C6PE00258105.html

3. Akdemir, A.: Research on task discovery for transfer learning in deep neural networks. In: Proceedings of the 58th Annual Meeting of the Association for Computational Linguistics: Student Research Workshop, pp. 33–41 (2020)
4. Wu, J.L.: Patent quality classification system using the feature extractor of deep recurrent neural network. In: 2019 IEEE International Conference on Big Data and Smart Computing (BigComp), pp. 1–8. IEEE (2019)
5. Banea, C., Mihalcea, R., Wiebe, J., et al.: Multilingual subjectivity analysis using machine translation. In: Proceedings of the 2008 Conference on Empirical Methods in Natural Language Processing, pp. 127–135 (2008)
6. Pan, S.J., Yang, Q.: A survey on transfer learning. IEEE Trans. Knowl. Data Eng. **22**(10), 1345–1359 (2009)
7. Xu, Q., Yang, Q.: A survey of transfer and multitask learning in bioinformatics. J. Comput. Sci. Eng. **5**(3), 257–268 (2011)
8. Weiss, K., Khoshgoftaar, T.M., Wang, D.D.: A survey of transfer learning. J. Big Data **3**(1), 9 (2016)
9. Yosinski, J., Clune, J., Bengio, Y., et al.: How transferable are features in deep neural networks? Advances in Neural Information Processing Systems, pp. 3320–3328 (2014)
10. Tohompson, C., Califf, M.E., Mooney, R.: Active learning for natural language parsing and information extraction. In: Proceedings of the 16th International Conference on Machine Learning, pp. 406–414. Morgan Kaufmann, San Francisco (1999)
11. Tong, S., Koller, D.: Support vect or machine active learning with applications to text classification. J. Mach. Learn. Res. **2**, 45–66 (2001)
12. Settles, B.: Active Learning Literature Survey. University of Wisconsin-Madison Department of Computer Sciences (2009)
13. Li, J., Xiao, Y., Hao, Z., Ruan, Y., Zhang, L.: Multi-example and multi-tag active learning based on SVM. Comput. Eng. Des. **37**(01), 254–258 (2016)
14. Zhou, Z., Shin, J., Zhang, L., et al.: Fine-tuning convolutional neural networks for biomedical image analysis: actively and incrementally. In: Proceedings of the IEEE Conference On Computer Vision And Pattern Recognition, pp. 7340–7351 (2017)
15. Zhu, J.J., Bento, J.: Generative adversarial active learning (2017). arXiv:1702.07956
16. Konyushkova, K., Sznitman, R., Fua, P.: Learning active learning from data. In: Advances in Neural Information Processing Systems, pp. 4225–4235 (2017)
17. Devlin, J., Chang, M.-W., Lee, K., Toutanova, K.: BERT: Pre-training of Deep Bidirectional Transformers for Language Understanding (2018)
18. Hochreiter, S., Schmidhuber, J.: Long short-term memory. Neural Comput. **9**(8), 1735–1780 (1997)
19. Amine, B.M., Mimoun, M.: Wordnet based cross-language text categorization. In: 2007 IEEE/ACS International Conference on Computer Systems and Applications, pp. 848–855. IEEE (2007)
20. Gliozzo, A., Strapparava, C.: Cross language text categorization by acquiring multilingual domain models from comparable corpora. In: Proceedings of the ACL Workshop on Building and Using Parallel Texts, pp. 9–16. Association for Computational Linguistics (2005)
21. Bel, N., Koster, C.H.A., Villegas, M.: Cross-lingual text categorization. In: International Conference on Theory and Practice of Digital Libraries, pp. 126–139. Springer, Berlin (2003)
22. Beltz, H., Rutledge, T., Wadhwa, R.R., et al.: Ranking algorithms: application for patent citation network. Information Quality in Information Fusion and Decision Making, pp. 519–538. Springer, Cham (2019)
23. Zeiler, M.D., Fergus, R.: Visualizing and understanding convolutional networks. In: European conference on computer vision, pp. 818–833. Springer, Cham (2014)

Construction of Unsupervised Prose Text Emotional Lexicon Based on Multidimensional Fusion

Kai Zhang[1,2(✉)], Jianshe Zhou[1,2], and Su Dong[1,2]

[1] Capital Normal University, 105 West Third Ring Road North, Haidian District, Beijing, China
irs_zhangkai@163.com
[2] Research Center For Language Intelligence of China, 105 West Third Ring Road North, Haidian District, Beijing, China

Abstract. Affective computing is an important tool for language processing and opinion mining, and emotional lexicon is the basis of emotional computing, and prose accounts for a large proportion in Chinese teaching and application in China. The construction of special emotional lexicon for prose language learning and language understanding is of great significance to the development of machine assisted human language learning and the improvement of machine deep reading comprehension. Therefore, the research on the construction of prose emotional lexicon is of great significance and value. In this paper, with the help of data collection tools, more than 27000 pieces of modern famous prose database are constructed. After preprocessing the data, denoising, deleting and selecting are completed to determine the walk set. Compared with PMI and word2vec, the accuracy of the method is improved by 16% and 14.8%, which proves that the comprehensive vector space can effectively improve the emotional vocabulary recognition of prose. Finally, 12762 prose general emotional lexicon is formed with the help of this method.

Keywords: Prose emotional lexicon · Prose reading comprehension · Random walk · Word vector · Word co-occurrence

1 Introduction

There has been no definite conclusion on the definition of prose. So far, it is difficult for prose to turn "category" into "body", which is even more difficult in Chinese education. In China's basic education stage, prose learning accounts for a prominent proportion. The number of prose in junior high school Chinese textbooks accounts for "half of the country", which is the most important part of textbook selection. As a literary style, it has its own unique teaching value, which has an indelible role in middle school students' Chinese learning [1]. Senior high school Chinese textbooks are composed of novels, dramas, poems and essays. Taking PEP senior high school Chinese compulsory textbook as an example, according to statistics, there are 65 texts and 11 essays, accounting for 17% [2].

Y. Weng et al. (Eds.): TridentCom 2020, LNICST 380, pp. 134–145, 2021.
https://doi.org/10.1007/978-3-030-77428-8_11

Prose is a literary genre with ideological, narrative and aesthetic features [3]. Compared with other literary styles, prose is more complex, and its emotional expression is particularly profound and changeable, which is a great challenge to the study of prose text understanding. Emotional words are one of the representative research contents in the field of artificial intelligence [4]. Emotional words in prose contain the author's rich emotional information, which plays an important role in prose text understanding. A good emotional lexicon is an indispensable foundation for emotional analysis [5]. The construction of an emotional dictionary in the field of prose can help computers better identify and understand the expression of emotions in prose, and improve the efficiency and accuracy of prose machine understanding.

2   Literature Review

Emotional dictionaries can be divided into general affective dictionaries and domain affective dictionaries. At present, most general affective dictionaries are constructed manually [6]. The more famous English emotion dictionaries are Sentiwordnet, General Inquire and Opinion Lexicon, while the Chinese ones are HowNet, DUTIR, NTUSD, etc. The construction of a general emotional dictionary manually annotates words by mining the synonymous, antonymy and hyponymy relations between words. The construction of general emotional dictionary is more dependent on the integrity of semantic knowledge base [7].

At present, there are relatively few standard Chinese emotion dictionaries. There are three open emotion dictionaries in Chinese information processing. HowNet emotional lexicon is the earliest and most widely spread. There are 4569 and 4370 commendatory and derogatory words in Chinese. The emotional lexicon of Dalian University of technology is divided into 7 categories and 21 sub categories according to the types of parts of speech, emotional categories, emotional intensity and polarity. The emotional intensity is divided into five grades: 1, 3, 5, 7 and 9. 9 indicates the strongest intensity, with a total of 27466 emotional words. There are 11171 Chinese affective dictionaries constructed by Taiwan University. The existing general Chinese emotional lexicon can not accurately judge the author's emotional inclination in the prose environment, and the artificial construction of emotional lexicon consumes a lot of human and material resources, so it is particularly important to automatically build a specific emotional lexicon around Chinese prose. At present, there are three kinds of methods for automatic construction of emotional lexicon: Based on semantic lexicon, based on corpus [8] and the combination of the two [4].

By mining the relationship between words through semantic dictionary database, we can construct emotion dictionary. Rao D et al. [9] extracted positive and negative affective words from WordNet by means of semi-supervised learning method and by giving positive and negative seed sets and synonym graphs. Hu M et al. [10] take adjectives as the research object, construct a seed set of positive and negative emotional words manually, and expand the emotional lexicon through the synonymy and antonymy of words in WordNet, and finally form a large-scale emotional dictionary. Strapparava C et al. [11] added some parts of speech such as nouns, verbs and adverbs on the basis of Hu M, and proposed a comprehensive emotion dictionary based on WordNet under the influence of multi part of speech. Choi Y [12] proposed a sentiment word construction algorithm based on the perception layer of FrameNet. Jia L [13] used Russell's (1980) model to capture the emotional vocabulary of online social media by deleting low-frequency and non emotional words and retaining repeated words.

Conjunctions and co-occurrence are commonly used in the construction of emotional lexicon based on corpus [6]. The method of conjunctions uses different meanings of conjunctions to construct emotional lexicon. The specific ideas are as follows: the emergence of inflectional words usually represents the change of emotional polarity, which will produce different emotional words, while the juxtaposed conjunctions represent the progressive connection of emotions and usually produce words with the same or similar emotions. Word co-occurrence method means that if two words often appear at the same time, it indicates that the emotional polarity of the two words is similar, so as to judge the emotional similarity between words.

However, in the field of discourse, such as prose, the use of words is flexible, and it is not enough to judge the emotional polarity of words only by conjunctions. However, the deficiency of Chinese semantic knowledge and the limitation of domain make the method based on semantic lexicon perform poorly in constructing domain oriented emotion dictionary. The combination of corpus and semantic knowledge can improve the accuracy of emotion tagging. The typical method is the semi-supervised relation graph method [14,15], which uses the semantic relations in the existing general emotional dictionaries to construct the relationship graph between words, and then uses a graph propagation algorithm to iteratively deduce the emotional tendency of the unknown polarity sentiment words in the corpus, so as to construct a relatively perfect domain emotion dictionary. Bing W et al. [16] proposed an unsupervised emotion classification method based on multi-level fuzzy calculation and multi criteria fusion. The self supervised learning fuzzy classification using labeled training data achieves good experimental results.

3   Design of Construction Method of Prose Emotion Dictionary

This paper proposes an unsupervised construction method of prose emotional lexicon based on multidimensional fusion. Through the data collection of prose website, the basic corpus is collected, and the emotional lexicon of Dalian University of Technology (7 categories, 21 sub categories, 27466 emotion words) is set as the basic emotional lexicon. After de-noising and processing the corpus, multi strategies are integrated to form a seed set. By constructing point mutual information (PMI), word contribution of word vector (word2vec) and joint semantic vector of semantic information of prose text, a comprehensive vector space based on prose corpus is formed. Finally, the random walk strategy is used to obtain the candidate sentiment word set which is similar to or similar to the seed set. And the sentiment lexicon in prose field is completed by using classification algorithm. According to the implementation method of this paper, the main construction process is as follows, as shown in Fig. 1.

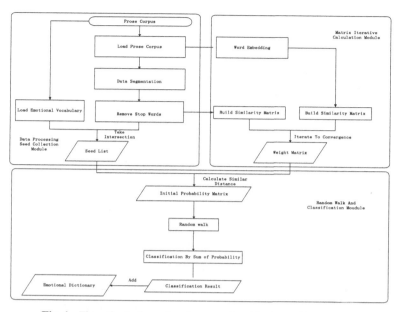

Fig. 1. Flow chart of constructing emotional lexicon of prose text.

The construction process is as follows:

(1) Data preprocessing. It mainly includes the acquisition and selection of prose corpus and the integration of existing emotional dictionaries to form a seed set.

(2) Word vector construction. The word2vec model in deep learning is used to transform words into word vector space, which lays the foundation for subsequent classifiers.

(3) Synthesis vector space classifier design. Through the prose corpus prepared by the author and the emotion dictionary after fusion, the training corpus is constructed. At the same time, the word vector model is used to transform words into comprehensive vector space, and network training is used to generate emotion classifier.

(4) The construction of emotional lexicon is commonly used in prose. The emotion dictionary in the field of prose is mainly composed of two parts: fusion emotional lexicon and candidate emotional lexicon. The classifier model is used to classify and judge its emotional polarity, and finally the common emotional lexicon in the field of prose is obtained.

3.1 Corpus Preprocessing

This study focuses on prose and needs a large number of prose corpus. This paper designs to use the network collection tools to obtain the current network common prose corpus as the candidate corpus. The specific design and collection of prose corpus are shown in Table 1.

It can remove duplicate data and filter ancient poetry. Finally, the collected results are merged into a semi-structured XML document of prose text corpus. The structure contains topics, authors and text. The database collects 27674 masterpieces. The experiment

Table 1. List of collection seed sets of prose corpus.

No.	Name	Link
1	Modern Prose Net	https://www.sanw.net/
2	China Prose Website	https://www.cnprose.com/
3	China Beautiful Article Net	https://www.sengzan.com/
4	Beautiful Article Net	https://www.748219.com/
5	Text Abstract Web	https://www.szwj72.cn/
6	Everyday Beautiful Article Net	https://www.365essay.com/
7	Classic Beautiful Article Website	https://meiwen.ishuo.cn/
8	Short Literature	https://www.duanwenxue.com/
9	Prose Net	https://www.sanwen.net/
10	99 Article Website	https://www.jj59.com/yuanchuang/
11	Prose Online	https://sanwenzx.com/index.html
12	Love net	https://www.biib.cn/
13	Easy Prose Reading Website	https://www.cnease.cn/index-htm-m-bbs.html

uses Python's beautiful soup library to complete the analysis, uses Jieba word segmentation and completes the stop word operation through the Harbin Institute of technology's stop list, and obtains 9449438 prose corpus. A total of 7012 affective words were selected from the intersection of the thesaurus and the Chinese emotional vocabulary ontology database (Dalian University of Technology). After classifying the emotional lexicon into seven categories: sadness, evil, good, surprise, fear, anger, and happyness, 10 emotion words were randomly mapped and selected as seed sets.

3.2 Lexical Relevance Analysis of Prose Corpus

By analyzing the content of prose corpus, it is easy to get that the words in prose are more implicit and profound in expressing emotions. All scenery words are emotional words, and different scenes express different emotions. Generally, not only adjectives express the author's emotion, but also the collocations of adverbs and adjectives contain emotional tendency. The connection of emotional words in prose and the rules that prose writers want to express their emotions are largely implied in the corpus. Therefore, if we want to obtain the emotional words, we need to consider the correlation between prose words.

PMI (pointwise mutual information) is a special case in NMI (normal mutual information), and NMI is a concept derived from information theory, which is mainly used to measure the degree of correlation between two signals. PMI is used to calculate the degree of correlation between two words in text processing. Compared with traditional similarity calculation, the advantage of PMI is to find out whether there is semantic correlation or topic correlation between words by finding the cooccurrence of words from the statistical perspective.

Definition 1: Co-occurrence calculation (G_PMI) uses the mutual information between any candidate words to measure the correlation between words. Assuming that the candidate lexicon is C, w_i and $w_j(i, j \subset C)$ is calculated as follows:

$$G\_pmi = \log(\frac{p(w_i, w_j)}{p(w_i) * p(w_j)}) = \log(\frac{p(w_i|w_j)}{p(w_i)}) = \log(\frac{p(w_j|w_i)}{p(w_j)}) \tag{1}$$

If w_i and w_j are distributed independently, then $p(w_i, w_j) = p(w_i) * p(w_j)$, which means $pmi(w_i, w_j) = \log 1 = 0$. On the contrary, if the distribution between w_i and w_j are not independent, then $p(w_i, w_j) > p(w_i) * p(w_j)$, and as the relevance is increased, the value of pmi is greater, which lead us to the conclusion that the more information w_i and w_j carry together, the more easier they will appear together.

Learning semantic knowledge by an unsupervised way in a large number of prose corpora is of great significance to the construction of prose emotional lexicon. At present, the commonly used method is to use vectors to represent semantic relations, Word2Vec uses word vectors to represent the semantic information of words by learning the text, in other words, through an embedding space to make words, which are semantically similar, close in the space. Therefore, this article uses the Word2Vec model to construct the prose vocabulary semantic network.

Definition 2: The semantic word vector space C_w2v is used to represent the contextual semantic relationship between words. The method is to embed a space, which is low-dimensional, to make semantically similar words very close in the space.

$$C\_w2v = \sum_{k=1}^{n} S(x_i, x_j) = \frac{\sum_{k=1}^{n}(x_{ik}x_{jk})}{\sqrt{\sum_{k=1}^{n} x_{ik}^2}\sqrt{\sum_{k=1}^{n} x_{jk}^2}} \tag{2}$$

$x_i \in R, x_j \in R$, R is the corpus set, and the dimension is n-dimensional, at which the larger the $s(x_i, x_j)$, the greater the similarity between the two words. Skip-gram is an unsupervised learning method that can be used for any original text. Compared with other word-to-vector expressions, it requires less memory. Only two weight matrices with dimensions [N, |v|] instead of [|v|, |v|] are needed. However, the calculation of the Softmax function of this model is time-consuming.

Definition 3: By Definition 1 and Definition 2, the co-occurrence relationship calculation G_pmi and the semantic word vector space C_w2v can be obtained respectively. In order to integrate the co-occurrence calculation and the semantic word vector space, the comprehensive vector space E (G_pmi, C_w2v) is specially defined.

$$\text{Vertical iteration}: E_v(t + 1) = \partial \times S \times E_V(t) + (1 - \partial) \times C_{w2v} \tag{3}$$

$$\text{Horizontal iteration}: E_h(t + 1) = \partial \times E_h(t) \times S + (1 - \partial) \times E_v^* \tag{4}$$

As mentioned above, the ∂ is the propagation parameter, and $\partial \in (0, 1)$, $E_v(0) = D$, the matrix is $S \subset R^{m \times m}$, $S = Z^{-1/2}G\_pmiZ^{-1/2}$

Firstly, by using Definition 2 to continuously iterate to get the adjacency column matrix E_v^*. Then the horizontal iteration is carried out until it tends to be stable, and get the adjacency matrix E_h^*. Finally, the integrated vector space E is obtained.

3.3   The Construction of Common Emotional Word Database in Prose

The random walk model [17] describes the correlation between candidate words through the connectivity between points, the model falls into two categories, random walk graph and random walk process. The random walk process is based on the random walk graph, setting out from the word x of unknown emotional tendency, then starting to walk, among all the words connected to the word x, if a word is more closer to the word x on the model graph, then the probability of getting to this word will be greater, and vice versa. Briefly speaking, the connection probability between points is used to measure the random walk correlation between words, which is suitable for the global exact minimum and the opposite of gradient descent.

For the $\forall x$ in the graph, which jumping to any vertex $\forall y$ with probability p(x, y), the p(x, y) is called the jumping probability. The walking process requires 4 input parameters, adjacency matrix E_h^*, initial probability distribution vector S_0, jump occurrence weight β and random jumping probability p. The random process iteration formula is as follows:

$$S_i(t + 1) = (1 - \beta) \times E_h^* \times S_i(t) + \beta \times p \ (0 < \beta < 1) \tag{5}$$

The vector $S_i(0)$ is the initial probability distribution from the word X_i to the seed set, m is the number of seed sets. Through the iteration of formula (3), a stable probability distribution S_i* can be obtained, and then the probability distribution of each type of seed set is calculated and the maximum class probability is obtained, that is, the maximum is taken after the sum of each seed probability of the type of seed set.

$$O(x_i[c]) = \underset{0<c<8}{\arg\max} \sum_{j=1}^{n} x_{ij}[c] \tag{6}$$

Among them, $O(x_i[c])$ represents the probability from the word x_i to the largest seed category C, and C represents the seed category, which is taken $c \in (0, 8)$ here, since the emotional word category is divided into seven categories, j represents the seeds in the seed set $j \in (1,n)$, and the n represents the number of seeds in each category.

4   Experimental Results and Analysis

According to the construction process of prose emotional lexicon as shown in Fig. 1, the server is configured as Intel (R) Xeon (R) Gold 5118 CPU @ 2.30 GHz, memory 256G.

4.1 Experimental Results of Data Preprocessing

After collecting the link organization in Table 1, 27674 famous prose works were obtained after de duplication and filtering. After word segmentation and elimination of stop words, 4718244 were obtained and 77389 were de duplicated. The thesaurus is deleted according to the frequency of words, and 10 times is selected as the threshold. The candidate word sequence is obtained by taking the intersection with the Chinese emotional vocabulary ontology database (Dalian University of technology emotional lexicon), with a total of 7012 emotional words. According to this candidate sequence, the sentiment types and parts of speech are analyzed as follows (Fig. 2 and Table 2):

Table 2. Analysis of emotional types and part of speech distribution of candidate word.

No.	Classification	Numbers	No.	Classification	Numbers
1	Happiness	656	1	Noun	2591
2	Evil	2244	2	Verb	2879
3	Good	3167	3	Adjective	1210
4	Grief	522	4	Adverb	128
5	Fear	275	5	Other	204
6	Surprise	66			
7	Anger	82			

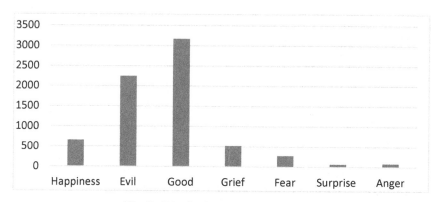

Fig. 2. Distribution of emotional words.

According to the analysis of the above results, the good and the evil are the same in the prose corpus, and there are few articles about anger. From the candidate parts of speech, verbs and names are more distributed. In order to balance the number of different kinds of seed sets, good experimental results are achieved. According to the above experimental data, the number of seed sets was selected. The accuracy rate (P), recall rate (R) and F1 value were used to evaluate the experimental results.

Table 3. Comparison experiment of seed set number selection.

The number of seed words	Accuracy	Recall	F1 value
6	35.3%	38.2%	36.1%
8	49.1%	49.7%	40.4%
10	56.8%	51.6%	55.4%
12	53.2%	50.6%	51.3%
14	51.4%	52.6%	50.7%

According to the experimental results of Wang [4] and others on low-frequency words, we combine the experimental results in Table 3. The analysis shows that the accuracy rate, recall rate and F1 value are the optimal solutions when there are 10 kinds of seed set respectively. Therefore, after mapping the emotional lexicon into seven categories: sadness, evil, good, surprise, fear, anger, and happiness, 10 emotion words are randomly selected as seed set (Table 4).

Table 4. Seed set of each emotion label in the random walk model

No.	Category	Seed set
1	Grief	血癌, 渺茫, 落难, 怏怏, 挫败, 变迁, 倾家荡产, 瘦瘠, 断气, 道别, 遇害
2	Evil	闪失, 不良, 旷日持久, 违反, 失禁, 驱使, 失效, 烦躁, 诬告, 喝斥
3	Good	振奋人心, 飘逸, 财礼, 标致, 憨笑, 亲历, 孝子, 见义勇为, 晶亮, 回报
4	Surprise	突如其来, 不期而然, 怔住, 惊天动地, 大吃一惊, 目瞪口呆, 奇特, 奇怪, 轰动, 天崩地裂
5	Fear	急切, 急如星火, 囚笼, 汗流满面, 危机四伏, 慌乱, 心悸, 交战, 汗颜, 扑腾
6	Anger	赌气, 怒冲冲, 不甘示弱, 惩治, 咆哮, 气急败坏, 泄愤, 可气, 疾言厉色, 针锋相对
7	Happiness	秋波, 水落石出, 朝阳, 尽意, 欢欣鼓舞, 启示, 启发, 畅顺, 畅所欲言, 盈余

4.2 Vocabulary Relevance Experiment of Prose Corpus

In order to achieve the goal of constructing prose emotional lexicon effectively and automatically, three groups of comparative experiments are designed to verify the accuracy and scalability of the method. According to the definition of correlation analysis in 3.2, G_ pmi, C_ w2v, E(G_ pmi, C_ W2v) can be obtained, it is co-occurrence relation matrix, semantic word vector space and comprehensive vector space.

According to the experimental results of the three methods, the methods are evaluated from the recognition accuracy of prose emotional lexicon and the classification accuracy of emotional words. The evaluation was carried out by random sampling method. Multiple groups of comparisons were set and the final mean value was taken as the global effect.

Classification accuracy of prose emotional lexicon: according to the results of the three methods, 30 emotion types were randomly selected from each category, and 7 groups of 30 words in each group were constructed as evaluation samples. After judging whether the sample belongs to the corresponding emotion category, the probability is obtained. $p(i) = \frac{q}{m}$, i is the type of emotion, q is the correct number of recognition, m is the number of samples.

Table 5. Accuracy evaluation of emotional lexicon classification in prose

Algorithm	Happiness	Anger	Grief	Good	Surprise	Fear	Evil
C_w2v	24.8%	10.7%	20.2%	30.9%	13.7%	30.7%	16.5%
G_pmi	20.6%	10.4%	17.8%	20.6%	17.8%	7.9%	10.3%
E (G_pmi,C_w2v)	**42.7%**	**32.3%**	**37.8%**	**47.5%**	**44.2%**	**39.9%**	**35.8%**

As can be seen from Table 5, the classification accuracy of emotion words in this paper has been significantly improved in seven dimensions. The second is C_W2v method, PMI method is the worst. It can be seen that in the field corpus such as prose, emotional expression is more diversified, rhetorical devices are widely used, and semantic similarity can effectively improve the identification of emotional words.In addition, the accuracy rate of "anger" in emotion category is low, which is due to the close relationship between "sadness" and "surprise". For example, "mourning without dispute" has both anger and sadness, resulting in the low accuracy of recognition.

The accuracy rate of emotional lexicon recognition: from the three groups of experimental results, 100 emotion words were randomly selected according to 5 groups. Through the evaluation of the results, we can judge whether they are emotional words. $p(k) = \frac{q}{m}$, k represents the group, q is the correct number of recognition, and m is the number of samples. Finally, the average value of the accuracy rate is calculated as the evaluation of the overall accuracy effect of this method.

Table 6. Evaluation of the recognition accuracy of prose emotional lexicon.

Algorithm	Group 1	Group 2	Group 3	Group 4	Group 5	Average
C_w2v	30.9%	39.4%	24.3%	32.8%	32.9%	32.0%
G_pmi	40.1%	32.5%	35.2%	29.7%	28.8%	33.2%
E (G_pmi,C_w2v)	47.6%	42.7%	45.1%	53.5%	51.3%	**48.0%**

It can be seen from Table 6 that the average recognition accuracy of PMI's prose emotional lexicon is higher than that of word2vec, which indicates that the co-occurrence of words in prose genre can better reflect the relevance between words, and it plays a greater role in the identification process of prose emotional words. The comprehensive vector space strategy proposed in this paper can effectively integrate the advantages of the two. With the help of random walk strategy, the local optimal solution is obtained, which is the overall optimal emotion word recognition effect, and the recognition effect is improved by 14.8%.

From the result table of correct emotion words, we can see that the highest number of emotion words identified by this algorithm is 12762, 10433 are identified by PMI, and 6824 are identified by word2vec. To sum up, PMI is better than word2vec in emotional word recognition, but it is not as accurate as word2vec in the classification and recognition of emotional words. From the experimental results, the proportion of "happy" and "good" texts is larger. At the same time, in the prose corpus the emotional color of the text is mostly commendatory, expressing positive emotions, or expressing sad emotions, with less other types.

5 Summary

In this paper, a domain corpus was constructed by proses. Firstly, the cohesion between words is fully considered. Secondly, the seed set is selected randomly by analyzing the category, part of speech and frequency of emotional words. Thirdly, the co-occurrence degree is constructed by PMI and word2vec algorithm respectively G_pmi matrix and C_w2v matrix. Then, the synthesis vector space E is constructed. After data validation, the method has good discrimination effect, effectively constructs the field corpus of prose field, and the experimental results verify the effectiveness of the proposed method.

Prose expresses the author's true feelings, flexible writing style, more diversified forms of expression, more subtle and subtle emotional expression. Due to the differences in personality, life experience and life attitude, the emotional types and expression ways of writers often have their own characteristics. Therefore, it puts forward better requirements for fine classification of emotional lexicon. At the same time, the use of rhetorical devices in prose is high. The machine understanding and processing of these rhetorical devices plays an important role in the automatic construction of emotional lexicon. For example, in Yu Dafu's autumn of the old capital, "I want to have a good taste of the 'autumn' of the old capital".

Therefore, the author of this paper will focus on the rhetoric recognition of prose and the detailed classification of emotional words in proses, so as to further enrich the emotional lexicon of prose and promote the discovery of new words and emotional connotation of prose emotional words.

Acknowledgement. This research was financially supported by "Research on key technologies and model verification of prose genre oriented text understanding (ZDI135–101)", "Research and Application of Key Technologies of Intelligent Auxiliary Reading System (ZDI135–79)", Capacity Building for Sci-Tech Innovation-Fundamental Scientific Research Foundation (20530290082).

References

1. Hui, G.: Junior High SchoolTextbook "Unified Edition" and "Curriculum Standard Edition" The Same Modern Prose Items Comparatively Study. Yan'an University (2020)
2. Lina, M.: Research on the Teaching Strategies of Modern and Contemporary Prose in Senior High Schools under the Background of New Curriculum Standards. Shaanxi Normal University (2019)
3. Zhaoshegn, W., Ping, H., Jiang, L.: The definition of prose. People's Daily Overseas Edition.
4. Suge, W., Qi, C., Xin, C.: Prose-oriented low-frequency emotion word extraction and emotion label determination. J. Shanxi Univ. (Nat. Sci. Ed.) **42**(02), 321–331 (2019)
5. Lili, M., Heyan, H., Xinyu, Z.: Overview of the construction of emotional dictionaries. J. Chin. Inf. Process. **30**(5), 19–27 (2016)
6. Ke, W., Rui, X.: A review of automatic construction methods for emotional dictionaries. Acta Automatica Sin. **42**(04), 495–511 (2016)
7. Fenglin, L., Yaxian, F.: Research on the Construction Method of Domain Emotion Dictionary. Libr. Theor. Pract. **2019**(12), 60-65+112 (2019)
8. Jiaheng, H., Yonghua, C., Chengyao, W.: Automatic construction of domain sentiment dictionary based on deep learning-take the financial domain as an example. Data Anal. Knowl. Disc. **2**(10), 95–102 (2013)
9. Rao, D., Ravichandran, D.: Semi-supervised polarity lexicon induction. In: Proceedings of the 12th Conference of the European Chapter of the Association for Computational Linguistics, DBLP 2009, Athens,Greece, pp. 675–682 (2009)
10. Hu, M., Liu, B.: Mining and summarizing customer reviews. In: Proceedings of the 10th ACM SIGKDD International Conference on Knowledge Discovery and Data Mining, pp. 168–177. ACM (2004)
11. Strapparava, C., Valitutti, A.: WordNet affect: an affective extension of WordNet. In: Proceedings of the 4th International Conference on Language Resources and Evaluation (2004)
12. Choi, Y., Wiebe, J.: +/−EffectWordNet: sense-level lexicon acquisition for opinion inference. In: Proceedings of the 2014 Conference on Empirical Methods in Natural Language Processing, pp. 1181–1191 (2014)
13. Zhao, J.L., Li, M.Z.: The development of the Chinese sentiment lexicon for internet. Front. Psychol. **10**, 2473 (2019). https://doi.org/10.3389/fpsyg.2019.02473
14. Fang, W., Yong, H.: Towards building a high-quality microblog-specific Chinese sentiment lexicon. Decision Support Syst. **87**, 39–49 (2016)
15. Khan, J., Lee, Y.-K.: LeSSA: a unified framework based on lexicons and semi-supervised learning approaches for textual sentiment classification. Appl. Sci. **9**(24), 5562 (2019). https://doi.org/10.3390/app9245562
16. Bing, W., Wei, H.: An unsupervised sentiment classification method based on multi-level fuzzy computing and multi-criteria fusion. IEEE Access **8**, 422–434 (2020)
17. Abdaoui, A., et al.: FEEL: a French expanded emotion lexicon. Lang. Resour. Eval. **51**(3), 1–23 (2017)

Algorithm Based on LL_CBF for Large Flows Identification

Lei Bai[1,2,3(✉)], Jianshe Zhou[1,2], and Yaning Zhang[1,2]

[1] School of Literature, Capital Normal University, Beijing 100048, China
[2] Research Center for Language Intelligence of China, Beijing 100048, China
[3] North China Institute of Science and Technology, Langfang 065201, Hebei, China

Abstract. In order to manage large-scale network, it is very important to measure and monitor the network traffic accurately. Identifying large flows timely and accurately provide data support for network management and network security, which has important meaning. Aiming at the deficiency of high false negative rate by using traditional algorithm to detect large flows, a novel scheme called LL_CBF is presented, which uses the policies of "separation of large flow filtering and large flow identification" to improve the accuracy of traffic measurement. The algorithm is improved from four aspects: large flows handled firstly, using counting bloom filter to filtrate most small flows, using least recent used mechanism to filter small and medium flows and pre-protect large flows, and using least elimination strategy to identify large flows. The theoretical analysis and the simulation result indicates that compared with the standard LRU algorithm and LRU_BF algorithm, our algorithm can identify the large flow in the network timely and accurately, and reduce the computing resource requirements effectively.

Keywords: Traffic measurement · Large flow · Least recent used · Least elimination strategy

1 Introduction

Accurately measuring and monitoring network traffic is the basis for managing large-scale networks. However, along with the rapid expansion of the Internet and the continual emergence of new applications, network traffic presents the characteristics of high speed, large scale and complexity, and the obvious feature is that the large amount of data generated and the high frequency of data packet arrival. This requires shorter data processing time than before, which brings great challenges to the storage capacity, processing capacity and transmission capacity of the network measurement system. Fortunately the flow-based measurement method opens up a new way for flow monitoring. By merging packets into the flow, the data volume is greatly compressed, making the storage, processing and transmission of network data easier. In network traffic measurement, a series of data packets that satisfy certain specifications are abstracted into a flow. According to this specification, some attributes of the packets are mapped into the flow to represent a unique identifier for the flow (flow ID). The most commonly used flow specification

Y. Weng et al. (Eds.): TridentCom 2020, LNICST 380, pp. 146–158, 2021.
https://doi.org/10.1007/978-3-030-77428-8_12

is the 5-tuple of the packet header (source/destination IP addresses, source/destination port numbers, and transport protocol).

Many studies show that the statistics of network flow present a strong heavy tailed distribution. Heavy tailed distribution is a probability distribution model, which means that in the statistical set, a small part of the elements have a very high frequency of appearance, occupying the vast majority of the set, and most of the elements appear at a very low frequency. This characteristic is called "the elephant and mice phenomenon", which means that most flows only have a small number of packets, while a small number of flows have a large number of packets. A notable feature of large flows is that they only account for a small part of the total traffic but generate the vast majority of the total traffic. So, in practical applications, in most cases, we only need to master large flow information to have an overall understanding of all network flows passing through the link which is convenient to manage and monitor the network traffic, and plays an important role in network traffic accounting, security detection, traffic control and other engineering applications. Therefore, how to use limited hardware resources to realize large flow identification has become a research hotspot in high-speed network measurement.

Traditional methods to achieve large flow identification needs to collect all packets in the network, and then extract their flow statistics, just as many previous studies have indicated. However, for the reason of system hardware computing speed and storage capacity is limited, and the network traffic data scale is huge, and the message arrival speed is extremely high, e.g. on the OC-768 (40 Gbps) backbone link, the average packet processing time is 8 ns. So, traditional methods have some flaws. In this paper, we propose and implement a new method called LL-CBF algorithm which use least obsolete (LEAST) & least recent used (LRU) & count bloom filter (CBF) algorithm to realize large flows identification.

The rest of this paper is organized as follows. Section 2 reviews related work. Section 3 introduces the traditional method of identifying large flows. Section 4 states the strategies used in our algorithm. In Sect. 5, we discuss how to identifying large flows by LL-CBF algorithm. Section 6 analyzes its performance theoretically. Experimental results on trace are presented in Sect. 7. Finally, Sect. 8 concludes the whole paper.

2 Related Work

Tatsuya Mori [1] described how to identify large flows through counting periodically sampled packets. Their key idea is to find the threshold of per-flow packets in sampled packets which can reliably indicate whether or not a flow is actually a large flow in not sampled packets and that such a threshold can be obtained based on Bayes' theorem. Kumar et al. [2] proposed a new technique referred to as space-code Bloom filter (SCBF) for extracting per-flow statistics of traffic in high-speed networks. Smitha Kim I [3] proposed LRU algorithm for identifying long-term high-rate flows at a router. Zhen Zhang [4] Used Bloom filter and LRU algorithm to realize long stream information statistics. ANTUNES N [5] estimate the tails of flow duration and size distributions under various sampling methods. Qingjun Xiao [6] proposed cardinality estimation solution mechanism to estimate large flows, which allocate each flow with a virtual estimator, and these virtual estimators share a common memory space. Aiping Zhou [7] design a new sketch data structure to detect network-wide persistent flow.

3   Classical Least Recent Used Algorithm

Least recent used (LRU) algorithm has a wide application in the computer field, such as database cache management, page management, disk cache management, etc. The fundamental of LRU is that always keeps the new element in the top of the cache and keep the least recent used element in the bottom. The LRU algorithm uses information about the pages accessed in recent past to predict the near future.

In an LRU cache every new entry is placed at the topmost position in the cache. The entry that was the least recently used is at the bottom. This is chosen to be replaced when a new entry has to be added and there is not enough space in the cache. This mechanism ensures that the recently used entries remain in the cache. The objective is to store state information for only large flows in the LRU cache. Smitha Kim I is the first to use LRU algorithm in traffic measurement. With a cache of limited size, a flow has to arrive at the router frequently enough to remain in the cache. Small flows are likely to be replaced by other flows fairly soon. These flows do not pump packets fast enough to keep their entries at the top of LRU list and hence become candidates for replacement. Large flows are expected to retain their entries in the LRU cache for long periods of time. However, when there are too many small flows or short-lived flows arrive at the cache suddenly, the large flows will be replaced by the small flows. This will decrease the accuracy of the measurement. To solve this problem we propose a new method.

4   Strategies Used in Our Algorithm

In order to solve the shortcomings of LRU algorithm that the small flows will replace large flows frequently, we improve the LRU algorithm from four aspects to improve the measurement accuracy.

4.1   Large Flows Handled Firstly

In order to identify large flows at the router, LRU algorithm must employ a cache which is of a fixed pre-determined size. For the reason of the number of memory we can afford is significantly smaller than the number of flows, when many small flows arrive at the cache suddenly, the large flows including the large flows that already identified will be replaced by the small flows.

To avoid this situation, we propose large flows handled firstly, which means that when a packet arrives, algorithm will validate whether this packet is belonged to a large flow which has been identified. If it is, then update the large flow information, if it is not, then packet will be handled later by other module. By this way, large flows which identified before will not be replaced by small one. By doing this can improve the measurement accuracy.

4.2   Using Counting Bloom Filter to Filter Most Small Flow Packets

Now that flow statistics has a characteristic which most small flows have a small number of packets, while a very few flows have a large number of packets. If we can filter out the packets of most small flows before they enter LRU cache, this will be reduce the number of flows which LRU algorithm handled, depress the probability of large flows replaced, and then will improve the accuracy of LRU algorithm.

Counting Bloom filter for representing a set $S = \{x_1, x_2......x_n\}$ of n elements is described by an array of m bits, initially all set to 0. It uses k independent hash functions with range $\{1,....,m\}$. CBF extend each unit in the standard Bloom Filter from a bit to a counter, so that it can add and delete elements. When adding an element, CBF uses k hash functions to map into the corresponding storage space and add 1 to the value of its mapped position; when deleting the element, the values of the corresponding k positions are reduced by 1.

The structure of CBF is shown in Fig. 1.

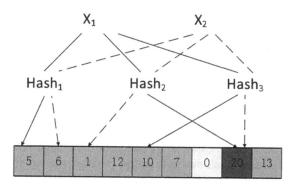

Fig. 1. CBF structure diagram

We use the characteristics of CBF to filter most small flows. When a packet arrives k hash functions are used to hash the flow ID of the packet which will be map into different positions of CBF. Since all packets belonging to the same flow will be mapped into the same location, the value of the large flow mapping location will be larger; for most small stream packets, the value stored in the mapping location is relatively small because of the different spatial locations of the mapping. By this way, most small flows can be filtered through the preset threshold n1, that is, when the value of the mapping position of the message is greater than or equal to n1, the message will be processed by the subsequent module. Most of the small flows are filtered out by CBF because they contain less packets and the value of mapping position is small. Due to the huge amount of data, there are also many small flows mapped to the same location, which leads to the small flows being submitted to the subsequent module for processing. Therefore, further processing of packets passing through the CBF is required.

4.3   Using the LRU Mechanism to Filter Small and Medium Flows and Pre-protect Large Flows

The LRU module is used to filter the middle and small flows passing through the CBF module, reducing the number of flows entering the LEAST module, thereby achieving pre-protection for large flows. The LRU maintains a cache and always keeps the flow which records of the latest arriving packets at the top of the LRU cache, while the longest unreachable flows are stored at the bottom of the cache queue. When a new flow reaches the LRU module through the CBF module, the LRU will create a new flow record and place it at the top of the cache. If the cache is full, the bottom flow will be replaced. Due to the short duration and the low arrival rate of the small flows, they are always possible to be replaced; while large flows tend to be stored at the top of the LRU cache because of their long duration and frequent access to the cache. The LRU is implemented as a doubly linked list. Each node contains an entry for flow id and the packet count. If the flow exists in the LRU linked list, put the flow at the top of the linked list; if a new flow arrives and the linked list is full, the bottom flow is eliminated and the new flow is placed at the top of the linked list. In order to make the search into the linked list easy, it is indexed by a hash table. Therefore, in addition to a small amount of additional operations due to hash conflicts, most objects only need to perform a hash operation to locate the flow record to which the message belongs.

However, due to the small storage space of LRU, when a large number of burst flows arrive or no new packets arrive in a short period of time, large flow objects may be eliminated by medium and small flows. Therefore, it is necessary to further use LEAST module to identify large stream objects.

4.4   Using LEAST Elimination Mechanism to Identify Large Flows

The LEAST module always eliminates the smallest flow and realizes long flow identification. If a packet arrives and its corresponding flow record is found in the LEAST table, then the size of the packet is added to this record; if the flow record corresponding to the packet is not in the LEAST table, then it will be mapped by the hash function To the corresponding items of CBF, and processed by CBF and LRU modules respectively. If the flow object passes the threshold set by CBF and LRU, a new entry will be added to the LEAST table to record the information of the flow. When the length of the LEAST table (the number of items stored) reaches the maximum, the smallest flow in the LEAST table will be eliminated in order to free up storage space for the newly arrived flow.

5   Identifying Large Flows by LL-CBF Algorithm

The large flow identification algorithm based on LL-CBF is composed of flow filtering function and flow identification function. The function of flow filtering is to filter out most of the small and medium flows information in network traffic, which is divided into two modules: CBF filtering and LRU filtering; the role of the LEAST module is to realize large flow detection. The pseudocode of the algorithm is described in Fig. 2 below.

```
initialize (CBF,LRU,LEAST)          //Initialize CBF,LRU,LEAST
While a packet x arrives
calculate H=h(1),h(2),...,h(k)       // Calculate k hash function values
if( isLargeFlows() ){      // If the large flow ID has already been identified
        update(count);              // Number of packets in the flow plus 1
}else{                              // Unrecognized flow ID
        CBF();                      // Call CBF function
}
CBF(){
        if  (any location of CBF[hᵢ(x)]ᵢ₌₁..ₖ<n₁){
                        //The k positions of CBF are all less than n₁
            add((CBF[hi(x)]i=1..k))    // CBF count plus 1
        }
        else       //The k positions of CBF are all greater than or equal to n₁
            LRU(x);                 // Call LRU function
}
LRU(x){
     if(find(x) or not full){
            // If already in the LRU linked list, or the linked list is not full
            update(count);          // Number of packets in the flow plus 1
            setTop();               // Put the flow node on top
            if (number(count)>=n₂)
                LEAST(x)
        }
        else               // Not in the linked list, and the linked list is full
            eliminate (last);           // Eliminate the last flow node
}
LEAST(x) {
     if(find(x) or not full){
            update (count);         // Number of packets in the flow plus 1
        }
        else               // Not in the linked list, and the linked list is full
            obsolete (minimum);     // Eliminate the smallest stream
}
```

Fig. 2. The pseudocode of LL-CBF algorithm

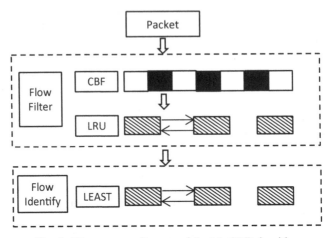

Fig. 3. The structure diagram of the LL-CBF algorithm

Figure 3 shows the structure diagram of the LL-CBF algorithm.

The procedure for identifying large flows by LL-CBF algorithm is enumerated as follows.

Step 1: First, when a packet arrives, k independent hash functions will compute k keys according to the 5-tuple identity (source/destination IP addresses, source/destination port numbers, and protocol).

Step 2: Secondly, validate whether this packet is belonged to a large flow. If it is, then the counter of large flow add one, if it is not, then packet will be handled by CBF.

Step 3: CBF validate whether the k positions of CBF are all less than n_1. If any of position is less than n_1, the counter of each position plus 1. Otherwise, the packet will be handled by LRU algorithm.

Step 4: LRU algorithm will search the cache to check if that flow's entry exists in the cache. On a miss, the flow is added to the cache if there is space in the cache. If there is no space in the cache, it replaces the least recently seen entry. It adds this entry in the topmost position in the cache. On a hit, update the entry in the cache. When the count of this flow exceeds the threshold n_2, this flow will be submitted to LEAST module.

Step 5: In LEAST module, LEAST algorithm will search the cache to check if that flow's entry exists in the cache. If find, then the size of the packet is added to this record; if not, it will determine whether the leap cache is full, if reaches the maximum size, the smallest flow in the LEAST will be eliminated, if not, then a new entry will be added to the LEAST table to record the information of the flow.

Step 6: At last, output the flows whose length is greater than the specified threshold TH which we recorded in LEAST, and those flows are large flows.

6   Performance Evaluation

The algorithm may have false positive during the large flow recognition process. False positive ratio (FPR) is the probability of identifying non large flows as large flows. In

CBF, the length of the counter array is m, the total number of detected packets is N, and all packets belong to n flows. When an element is inserted into the CBF, the probability that a certain position is mapped to is $1/m$, $n * k$ mappings were performed in total. The probability that the hash position is empty is P'

$$P' = \left(1 - \frac{1}{m}\right)^{kn} \approx e^{\frac{nk}{m}} \tag{1}$$

False positive ratio P

$$P = \left(1 - P'\right)^k \approx \left(1 - e^{\frac{nk}{m}}\right)^k = \exp\left(k\ln\left(1 - e^{\frac{nk}{m}}\right)\right) \tag{2}$$

Let

$$f(k) = k\ln\left(1 - e^{\frac{nk}{m}}\right)$$

When f takes the minimum value

$$\frac{\partial f(k)}{\partial k} = 0$$

Then

$$k = \ln 2\left(\frac{m}{n}\right)$$

So, the minimum value of CBF FPR is

$$P_{min} = \left(\frac{1}{2}\right)^k \tag{3}$$

In any measurement time period, the flow rate obeys the Pareto distribution with position parameter 1. Assuming that the total number of packets in the measurement period is M, the LRU creates a new flow identifier every N packet on average, and eliminate a flow at the bottom of the linked list. Suppose the size of a large flow F is exactly equal to the threshold TH, then the probability of no large flow F in N consecutive messages obeys the hypergeometric distribution.

$$\binom{TH}{0}\binom{M - TH}{N}/\binom{M}{N} \tag{4}$$

When $M \gg N$, formula (1) can be approximated as $\left(1 - \frac{TH}{M}\right)^N$. Therefore, the probability that the current F is eliminated is

$$P_{LRU}(F = TH) = P(F = TH)\left(1 - \frac{TH}{M}\right)^N \tag{5}$$

Since

$$P(F = TH) = \theta/TH^{\alpha+1}$$

Then

$$P_{LRU}(F = TH) = \frac{\theta}{TH^{\alpha+1}}\left(1 - \frac{TH}{M}\right)^N \tag{6}$$

In which θ is the normalized parameter.

$$\theta = \left(\sum_{i=1}^{M} i^{-\alpha-1}\right)^{-1}$$

Because the algorithm search process uses hash function set, the memory cost of one access to hash space is $O(k)$. At the same time, the LRU linked list uses doubly linked list, and the zipper method is used to resolve hash conflicts. The average search length of the algorithm is $O(1 + \beta/2)$, β is the filling factor.

7 Experimental Analysis

In order to verify the effectiveness of the LL_CBF algorithm, we use Trace collected from CAIDA for simulation experiments. There are 6187376 packets and 68367 flows in total. CBF uses $k = 6$ hash functions, and it's hash space is [0.. 65535]. The original distribution of network traffic is shown in Fig. 4. It can be seen from the figure that the distribution statistics of the network flow present a heavy-tailed distribution.

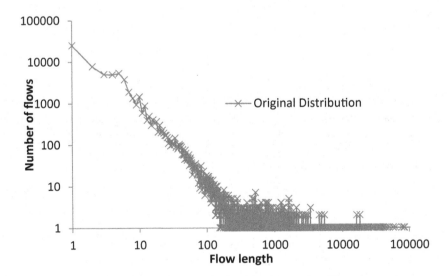

Fig. 4. The original distribution of network traffic

Figure 5 shows the comparison of whether the big flow is processed first. It can be seen from the figure that the measurement accuracy of large flow handled firstly is much higher than that of post handled. This is because the post-processing method will cause

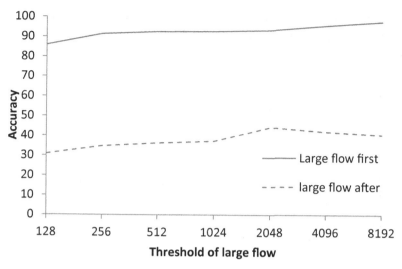

Fig. 5. Comparison of large flow pre-processing and post-processing

the large flows to be eliminated by the small flows, thus the measurement accuracy is reduced.

Figure 6 shows the proportion of the number of filtered flows when the CBF counter changes. The greater the value of counter, the more flows are filtered. As the counter value increases, most of the small flows are discarded because the value of the mapping position is smaller than the counter.

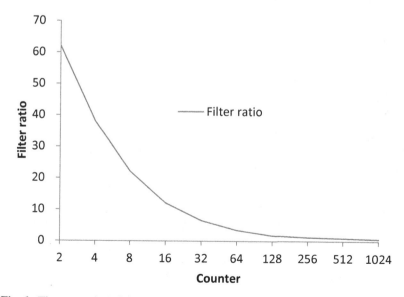

Fig. 6. The proportion of the number of filtered flows when the CBF counter changes

Figure 7 displays the measurement error when LRU cache space changes. The larger the cache space, the smaller the probability of the large flow being replaced and the higher the accuracy.

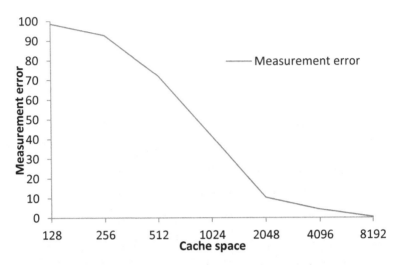

Fig. 7. Measurement error when LRU cache space changes

Figure 8 indicates the comparison of measurement accuracy between LL_CBF algorithm, the LRU_BF algorithm and the standard LRU algorithm, using the same hash function and number and cache space.

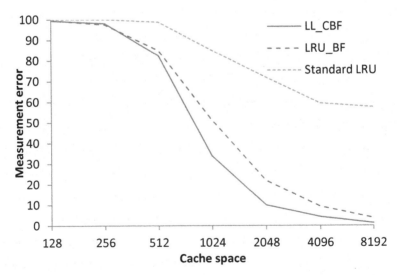

Fig. 8. Comparison of the accuracy of three algorithms for measuring large flow

Experimental results show that compared with the standard LRU algorithm and LRU_BF algorithm, the LL_CBF algorithm proposed in this paper has higher measurement accuracy, especially when the cache space is relatively small the advantage of the LL_CBF algorithm is more obvious. This is because when the cache is small, the standard LRU algorithm and the LRU_BF algorithm, for the cache space is full, a large number of newly arrived small flows will eliminate the unidentified large flows in the cache. However, the LL_CBF algorithm can filter out most of the small flows through the filtering mechanism, while retaining the identified large flow information, reducing the impact of the small flow on the large flow, thereby reducing the measurement error of the algorithm.

8 Conclusion

Due to the rapid and large-scale development of the network, it is becoming more and more difficult to completely measure network flow information online. In this paper, based on the measurement defects of the sudden large number of small flows that lead to the elimination of large flows and the characteristics of network heavy tail distribution, propose a large flow detection algorithm based on LL_CBF, which will filter out most of the small flow through filtering mechanism, and reduce the probability of small flows entering the cache space, realize the strategy of "grasp the big and let go of the small". The complexity and error rate of the algorithm are analyzed, and the effectiveness of the algorithm is verified by experimental data. The results show that compared with the standard LRU algorithm and LRU_BF algorithm, the new algorithm can identify the large flow in the network timely and accurately under the condition of using less storage space, and meet the actual measurement needs.

Acknowledgment. We would like to express our appreciation for the assistance with data collection we acquire from CAIDA. This research was financially supported by "Research on key technologies and model verification of prose genre oriented text understanding (ZDI135-101)", "Research and Application of Key Technologies of Intelligent Auxiliary Reading System (ZDI135-79)", Capacity Building for Sci-Tech Innovation-Fundamental Scientific Research Foundation (20530290082).

References

1. Tatsuya, M., Masato, U., Ryoichi, K.: Identifying elephant flows through periodically sampled packets. In: Proceedings of ACM SIGCOMM/IMC 2004, pp. 115–120. ACM Press, Taormina (2004)
2. Kumar, A., Xu, J., Wang, J., Spatschek, O., Li, L.: Space-code bloom filter for efficient per-flow trafficmeasurement. In: Proceedings of IEEE INFOCOM 2004, Hong Kong, China, (2004)
3. Kim, S.I., Reddy, N.A.L.: Identifying long-term high-bandwidth flows at a router. In: Proceedings of the 8th International Conference on High Performance Computing, Hyderabad, India, pp. 361–371 (2001)
4. Zhang, Z., Wang, B.: Traffic measurement algorithm based on least recent used and Bloom filter. J. Commun. **34**(1), 111–120 (2013)

5. Antunes, N., Pipiras, V.: Estimation of flow distributions from sampled traffic. ACM Trans. Model. Perform. Eval. Comput. Syst. 1(3), 1–28 (2016)
6. Xiao, Q., Chen, S.: Cardinality Estimation for Elephant Flows : A Compact Solution Based on Virtual Register Sharing. IEEE/ACM Trans. Netw. (TON) **25**(6), 3738–3752 (2017)
7. Zhou, A., Zhu, C.: Detection method for network-wide persistent flow based on sketch data structure. Comput. Appl. **39**(08), 2354–2358 (2019)

Author Index

Printed in the United States
by Baker & Taylor Publisher Services